A Home in the World

Martine and Caroline Laffon

A Home in the World
Houses and Cultures

Translated from the French by Lenora Ammon

Harry N. Abrams, Inc., Publishers

Contents

Yemen, Hadramawt
Valley, city of Shibam.
House towers, made of
mud bricks, built in an
ancient riverbed

Introduction

To know the history of humans it is important to look at their houses. Houses often tell what place the inhabitants give themselves in the universe, and how they set the boundaries of that universe. They disclose myths and beliefs, fears and means of self-protection, habits of meeting and communication. Houses reveal their inhabitants, complex relationships with earth, water, air, and light. They are cocoons made from minerals, animals, or plants. Their shapes draw circles, squares, rectangles, or even triangles on the landscape—geometric shapes that are adjusted to the needs of the human body. The body assigns a function to interior space and gives it a soul. Thus, in a subtle play and a secret intertwining, the cosmos encompasses the house and the house encircles beings.

Like a shell, the house can open to others, and like a fortress it can protect against them. But the walls carry traces. Their thickness, roughness, colors, and stains speak of time passed from birth to death. Allotted space changes with age, marital status, and sex. The orientation—facing or turning away from the entrance, toward or against the sun, cold, and wind—is not the same. And the imprint left by the body on the interior of the house follows this evolution. This is the way of life.

If houses fit into one another and the shapes of their roofs merge together, they show a common history echoed from house to house. No one would dare to transgress it by inventing another way of living. A village's founding ancestors hand down a respected know-how, and everyone who comes after them follows the rites of construction so that the harmony of the world and the benevolent peace of the gods are not disturbed. In the action of building one's house, an original story is replayed—whether it is simple or complex, remembered or forgotten. This original story is the foundation on which the house is built. It perpetuates the identity of a village, its customs and traditions. Thus, each house delimits a sacred space that a stranger cannot penetrate without being invited.

Talismans hanging at the door serve to stop misfortune right at the threshold and sickness at the barrier of the body. When celestial spirits want to enter, they pass through the opening in the roof, following the smoke's path. They will always be honored and have an important place in the house, if they bring what is needed for happiness, health, and prosperity. And if one day houses no longer have anything to say, nothing more to show, it will be because individuals no longer have dreams to inhabit them.

Building Your World

Where does the need to draw a border, define a space, and mark a beginning and an end come from? Since we cannot be constantly in motion, we choose places where we can stop in order to be alone, to be with our families, or to be with our fellow creatures. Such places are structured, organized, laid out, and decorated according to a culture's ideas and images regarding an acceptable spatial environment. These criteria vary greatly depending on the culture. Curiously, the act of clearing away a portion of the bush, appropriating it by working the soil for cultivation, raising certain species of animals, and supervising their movements changed many things: habitat, occupation of space, landscape, technique, social organization, art, and religion.

Archeological digs in the Middle East have uncovered the dwellings of a civilization extending from the Euphrates to

Nepal, Laprak, Gurung village. Houses built on the mountainside

the Sinai, dating back ten thousand years. The dwellings were true houses, half-buried in round pits, with walls reinforced by dry stone. Traces of one or two hearths and vestiges of poles, placed like spokes to support the roof, were found. Why did these people choose to settle here? Was it only a question of climate, natural resources, comfort, and safety? To understand what determined sites such as these and what determined the form of habitats built on them, we must ask ourselves how the individual perceived the connections with the group, what relationship there was with the surroundings and with natural phenomena, and what the links were between the visible and invisible worlds. To settle on a particular site and to build one's house there does not leave anything to chance. In many traditional cultures, villages follow the curves and slopes of the topography, resting on stilts for protection in the heart of the lush forest or the troubled water of a lagoon. Without taking possession of anything, the houses borrow from their environment what is needed for their construction while bonding with the landscape. Thus they follow the course of rivers, the roads of deserts, attach to the flanks of wind-swept mountains, and huddle for a while along the valley floor or the flat steppes, taking ever-vigilant care not to disturb the universal harmony.

As the great founding ancestors have transmitted, to in-habit nature one must not disrupt the connection from the hearth to the roof of the house, from the earth to the sky, from mortals to gods, and the comings and goings between them. Round, square, or triangular—the shapes of houses are determined according to varying conceptions of the world, mortals, and gods. Wisdom passed from generation to generation can best explain why houses are built in one particular space versus another that may be unfavorable. The rites of secular construction renew the initial act of the creator at the beginning of the world. By erecting the walls of their intimate space at the four corners of the horizon—tes-timonials to their life, birth, and death—mortals become like gods and houses, like fortresses against the oblivion of time.

Questions of Shape

To live in a landscape where the mineral world dominates, where grass and plants are rare to the point that the houses themselves seem aggregates of their environment, individuals need the experience of traditions tested by generations of builders. But why is a particular shape preferred? In the past, certain Mesopotamian, Egyptian, and Chinese cultures constantly opted for rectangular figures. Today in Africa, side by side in the same region, you can encounter buildings whose various shapes depend on whether the building is a granary or a hut. Does the function of a building determine its form? If the circular shape is only to retain heat from a low fire throughout the night, why is it found in both Arctic and tropical regions? And why are Inuit hunting shelters round, like those of the Pygmies?

In Siberia, dwellings can be changed architecturally to accommodate a person's sedentary winter lifestyle or a nomadic shepherd's summer routine. In a similar climate, the Samis and the Nenets fight the glacial cold, but their houses have nothing in common. The former build half-buried lodges of stone and peat, into which they enter through the roof. The latter put up tents made of a light wooden structure covered with several layers of animal skins. Elsewhere, depending on needs and on the topography of the landscape, a temporary shelter,

Turkey, Cappadocia.
Troglodytic houses

like a hut made of branches or an opening in a cliff face, can suffice for a few nights. The hut is burnt before leaving, unless it is abandoned to serve as a significant indicator of a passageway for other tribes.

Some building choices have natural explanations. The inhabitants of Dolpo build thick walls—using material that captures and retains heat—with a minimum of windows and only one door, which is itself protected by a wall. Obviously when you are more than 13,000 feet (4,000 meters) high on the Himalayan chain, it is best to live in buildings huddled close together to mitigate the ceaseless blowing of the wind. But why make rectangular houses with terraced roofs? Is it to accommodate the tent that is sometimes put up there in summer? Willow and juniper branches are placed on the roofs to stop rainwater from infiltrating; wouldn't a sloping roof be better adapted? And what can be said about the houses of the Boros of Amazonia, whose walls and roofs are covered with a thick layer of thatch that keeps the hot, humid air from circulating? The discomfort is acceptable if it can be justified by a higher value, like that of being protected from real dangers, or from dangers, anchored in the collective imagination, that arise from modifying the ancestral structure of the dwelling. Who would want to risk violating a taboo?

Côte d'Ivoire, Niofoin, Senufo village. A village of huts with pointed roofs made of millet stalks

Russia, Siberia.
Nenet camp of
reindeer-skin tents

Pitching Your Tent

Living in the desert, traveling, and searching for water holes is not a way of life that the nomads endure but a choice, a form of liberty, which is sometimes accompanied by contempt for those who are sedentary. Nomads come to terms with nature and mortals to survive and perpetuate their traditions. Endlessly menaced by drought, diseases that ravage their cattle, and plunderers, they invariably set up their black woven goat-hair tent at every campsite. Though waterproof—for the rare rain of the Saharan desert—and low—for protection against violent winds—the tents are poor heat insulators. Are they a habitat that is well adapted to this environment?

Who has made the Beni-Abbas of the Djurdjura Mountains build, for seven hundred years, Saharan houses with terraced roofs, on which snow accumulates in winter? Every spring the roofs have to be repaired. What makes the Samburus of Kenya enter bent over, through the only door of their houses— houses made of a single plant mass 13 feet (4 meters) high, houses that look like ant or termite hills? Although nature provides shapes that can be copied without a primary concern for comfort or functionality; and myths, traditions, and the sacred give lines and aesthetics to the imaginary, the myths are not shared, nor are the requirements of the gods and the climates. In China, the demiurge Yu is the great blacksmith and carpenter who traveled across nine mountains and nine rivers and divided the squared earth into nine regions. In India, the celestial builder measured the earth and, using a right-angled instrument, drew the square. The circle inscribed in a square, the mandala, represents the model plan of the perfect city. Thus the invisible frontiers between gods and mortals are marked out by the geometry of dwellings like their respective imprints in the landscape.

Center of the World

It is said that Cain, after murdering his brother Abel, pleaded with the biblical God to avoid making him a wanderer traveling over the earth. He became the first builder of a city, which he named after his son Enoch. Rome, with its seven hills, was built on the blood of another brother—Remus. He transgressed his twin's order prohibiting him from overstepping the furrow traced in the ground to mark the boundary of Romulus's city. The myths of cities' origins are often bloody, but they establish the adoption of a people's seden-tary lifestyle.

No doubt, dwelling within a square—a symbol of stability and fixedness—lends itself to a sedentary lifestyle, while setting up within a circle—a symbol of movement—is appropriate for nomadic cultures. While the capital is often considered the center, the pivot, the axis, even the navel of the world, in central Africa it is not a geometric shape that configures the city of Luanda, but a turtle—with a head, a tail, and two sides. Thus the city integrates the character of this animal drawn on the ground. Symbol of wisdom, cunning, resistance, and longevity, the turtle possesses virtues that are conferred to the reigning royal power. Each inhabitant knows his or her position on the turtle. The king is placed near the tail, the heir near the head, and all others according to an established order.

For the Saos of Chad, a legend also explains the plan of the city of Makari. A hunter who came from the East wanted to settle on land occupied by a couple of monitor lizards. The hunter respectfully gave them food and presented them with offerings, and

New Guinea, Trobriand Islands. Bird's-eye view of the village. The shapes of villages often mirror the mythologies of the inhabitants.

the monitor lizards finally gave him their land. Then, with his spear, he traced the boundaries of the city. Until the reign of the Serpent King, chiefs had rapidly followed one another, sometimes taking power after merciless combats. Although loved by the population, the Serpent King quickly became more and more demanding and even tyrannical. One day, two twin brothers, accompanied by their sister, came from a Muslim country and decided to kill him for the common good. They sliced off the head of the Serpent King; his intestines were thrown into the center of the city, and his body cut into eight pieces, which formed the districts of the city. Soon after, the eldest brother seized power. Therefore, according to Saos tradition, the city is a world within a world, and the individual, a world within the city.

The traditional villages of Mali also derive from a human form. The chief's hut represents the head, notables' and princes' huts signify the shoulders, and according to the social hierarchy, different families' huts form the sides of the body and the legs. In the belly of the village, where the central courtyard is located, servile classes live where slaves lived in the past. (Placed in the village interior, they were under high surveillance and could not escape.) The central square also functions as a meeting place where village problems are discussed, and conflicts resolved. Ritual rites are performed here. Each village is a sacred space. The initiated villagers bury talismans for protection from enemies, wildcats, and evil spirits at the village's entrance, center, and exit.

Namibia, Kaokoland Desert. The Himbas' huts, built of branches so they can be taken down quickly, fit the nomadic lifestyle.

China. Terraced rice fields.
Houses' orientations are
still determined with the
help of a geomancer.

Approved Sites

A village's location can often be explained by qualities such as sunlight, altitude, water sources, pastures, wind shelter, and impregnability or openness to trade. All these factors, validated by experience, doubtlessly affect the choice of certain locations. But curiously, other cultural, religious, magical, and sometimes irrational criteria seem just as decisive. Certain houses' orientations can seem contrary to common sense, though they have a decisive symbolic logic. Thus, for the Chams of Vietnam, dwellings are completely exposed to the torrid sun because the shade of the trees is considered an ill omen. On the other hand, some Cambodian tribes do not build near trees out of respect for them; it would be an ill omen for the roots to grow under a home. The Chinese peasants of the Guangzhou region, who try to capture the positive supernatural forces indispensable for social success, think it completely natural that trees filter them since these forces come from the water streaming from the hills. Before building a house it is necessary to plant corn and wait until it is high enough in order to benefit from its influence.

For tribal peoples of Thailand, ideal conditions have seemingly all come together: proximity to the jungle for wood, game, and wild plants; a water source; a slight slope; and cultivable land. However, this is not enough. The village chief and the elders ensure that the proprietary and guardian spirits of a new location are favorable. A hole is dug in the precise location of the future settlement, and four grains of rice are laid down around a center in a spokelike pattern. They symbolize the future dwellings and the center of the village. The grains are then covered with a bowl, and a few days later the chief and elders come to check that no grain of rice has been moved. If all grains remain intact, the site, chosen by mortals, is approved by the gods.

Cosmic Influence

A society's conception of the universe, the environment, and the cosmos determines different ways of living as much as choice of site does. For the Pawnee of North America, the location of one village in relationship to another mimicked the position of stars in the sky. For the Lao of Southeast Asia still, a village must not cut the curved path of the sun, since this brings misfortune. Main facades are located toward the rising sun, the east—the symbol of life—and away from the west—the symbol of death. In India, orientation toward the east is also imperative. Doors of houses built on a steep slope may open on the upward slope in respect of this belief, which makes it rather impractical to leave the house. In Japan, the cardinal points may be favorable or unfavorable. A southeasterly orientation is considered beneficial—even though in some regions typhoons arrive from this direction. For the Dogon of Mali, the location of farms and houses must follow the cosmic order. Villages are built in pairs representing the sky and the earth. The Kotokos of Cameroon think that the city is the reproduction of the world, with a south and a north pole, corresponding not to geographic points but to energy points. A city cannot be built without taking these principles into consideration. For the Yakuts of Siberia, the sky is a canvas stretched above the earth to protect it, and the best way to inhabit the landscape is to take shelter under a tent. This preserves the original harmony of nature. In some Pacific islands, it is the lines of universal force that determine the site.

This idea that nature and humankind form one body is found in the design of traditional villages, which merge with the landscape. The curves of the architecture are wedded to the contours of the terrain—a successful symbiosis of humans, the elements, colors, and building materials. Nothing disturbs the cosmic and aesthetic balance. The use of natural forms testifies that the human being is an integral part of the universe. Houses connected to each other by shape, and anchored to the landscape express a shared consciousness, a group commitment to ally with trees, rocks, sand, bumps, meandering streams, and land in a vision of the unity of the universe, the landscape, and humankind. One does not treat the site callously; one does not violate it but works with it because the world, the divine work, cannot be profaned.

Opposite: Mali, Dogon
country, Ireli. Millet
granaries erected on the
cliff, in harmony with the
landscape.

Following pages:
Afghanistan. A village
melted into the landscape,
near Sarobi

Building Elements

In the West, the Greek philosopher Empedocles based the universe on four elements: water, earth, air, and fire. Indispensable for life, they could work with or against each other. Other cultures, like China, thought that the world was composed of five elements: water, earth, fire, metal, and wood, whose interactions could be a source of happiness. Well before the discovery of the earth's magnetism, sages explained that invisible currents traveled through the ground. They were beneficial if they followed a meandering line, unlucky if they traveled a straight one. Therefore, building on flat and wet sites, near mountain torrents and—today—near railroad tracks or telephone lines was to be avoided. The practice of feng shui (literally "wind and water course") put the individual in harmony with nature. The foundation of cities, or of imperial residences, did not leave anything to chance.

Thus today in the Forbidden City, the administrative buildings are built in the south to be compatible with the fire element and the symbol of authority. The residences in the north correspond to the water element. The location of any construction depends on the symbolism of the elements, and even a building's dimensions are influenced by feng shui. To find the ideal place for lodgings, these rules must be taken into account: People must be protected from harmful influences from the north; a mountain or a symbolic representation, such as a mound in a garden, will achieve this. There must be running water in the east, a road in the west, and exposure to the sun in the south. The geomancers, also called "masters of fate," use a special compass to determine direction. It is out of the question to find a site and undertake construction without their advice. Their compasses always point to the south, direction of the sun, warmth, and life. All the elements that must be taken into account—such as the zodiac, the calendar, the yin and yang principles, the constellations, and the planets—are inscribed on the compass. Masons and artisans must also respect the principles of feng shui or risk exposing the property owner to catastrophe. Only the geomancer, in contact with supernatural forces, can find a countermeasure or remedy against evil spirits. The spirits move in a straight line, so doors in a row or long corridors must be avoided.

China, Guizhou-Guangxi Province, Dong minority. In the past, towns were built according to rules that were made to put humans in harmony with the five elements.

Indonesia, Siberut Island, Matotonan. Houses on pilings under the monsoon. A space is often reserved in the village for spirits and supernatural creatures.

Magic Corners

North, south, east, or west? It is good to know where to find invisible spirits. For the Luluas of Congo, the west is the place of evil spirits. On the other hand, the east, the heavenly place of the "village of sweet bananas" is the abode of positive forces. Without necessarily taking into consideration the cardinal points, the Akha people of Thailand prefer, according to the ethnologists Paul and Elaine Lewis, to clearly set the boundaries of the human kingdom and the spirit kingdom in order to avoid any problems. However, a myth recounts that long ago humans and spirits lived together in peace. Their good-neighbor relationship was complicated when the spirits began to steal eggs from villagers and villagers took the spirits' cucumbers. The conflict increased the thefts of one side from the other. Finally, it was better to live separately. The Akhas lived in the villages and the spirits, in the jungle. To ensure that one did not encroach on the domain of the other, "village gates" were built on each border. A crosspiece on two posts of wood designated each gate. Under no circumstances could these gates be touched by the villagers—and certainly not by a stranger. If the gates were tainted, a fine had to be paid toward the necessary offerings. These sacred gates still exist in Akha villages. The main gate protects from illness, wild cats, leprosy, vampires, and anything that is a threat to the village. Small wooden statues, often of a man and a woman, are placed at the foot of the gate; they clearly indicate the place where the human kingdom begins. The Akhas feel vulnerable when they are in the jungle—the spirit kingdom. Therefore, they pass through the village gate when they return as if through a decontamination screen.

In northern Nepal, the temples and sanctuaries are built in a "pure" space, above the world of men, out of respect for the Buddha. Having a divine nature, the Buddha can only be placed above human beings.

Exterior Signs

Whether a house is a shelter, refuge, or temple, its design expresses its culture's values and the social importance given to material comfort. While the West looks to a house for reinforced protection from their own kind—as a stable refuge from the hazards of life—the Japanese want a fragile, temporary structure close to nature, thus measuring the impermanence of all things. Anthropologists have suggested that building a house is not universal. In regions of the world such as Southeast Asia, South America, and Australia, tribes live without roofs over their heads while they erect sophisticated huts to serve as altars to the gods and their ancestors; for their own needs, they have chosen to build a kind of windscreen. Knowledge of building techniques is not the only explanation for different types of dwellings. The Egyptians knew how to construct an arch, but rarely used it. Social values such as prestige, power, and success can alter the number of stories in a house or replace the traditional thatch with galvanized sheet metal, but can social values modify form?

The French expression "to have a gable on the street," meaning to be prosperous and highly respected, can apply to many other cultures: the dwelling is so much an exteriorization of what the owner is or wants to appear to be. In Tibet, houses are made of stones cemented with clay. The cattle

India, Rajasthan, Thar Desert. Inhabited space is sometimes marked by a simple windscreen.

stay on the first floor, while the second floor is the living space. According to the degree of affluence, other floors can be added. The windows are painted on the outside, and the trapezoid shape of the house (with a wider base) is not exactly the same as that of ordinary houses, though the same materials are used.

For many years in West Africa, social success has required that traditional cob walls, a good insulator made of raw clay, be abandoned for cement blocks—which provide no heat protection. The Western architectural model, an exterior sign of wealth, disrupts the use of materials and the interior or exterior layout of houses. Large glass windows can transform a house into a real oven when temperatures are constantly near 92°F (34°C). These windows have replaced the small openings that let air circulate. Ways of arranging space send messages about the value a house represents in society. In Annam, a Chinese province, as soon as peasants get a little money, they build a house way above their means—not a very comfortable one. Thus it is said that "you can find more wealthy houses than wealthy families."

Afghanistan, Kundūz region. Round houses, made of mud, pierced with small openings to keep them cool

In Relief

In Mongolia a story recounts how three gods created the world. Two made the universe according to their idea: flat like a pat of yak dung. They settled there without concern for the opinion of the third god. When he demanded a space for himself, they refused. To avenge himself, he created a mountainous relief, upsetting their completely flat world. This was also how the *gher* (a small bump of white fabric placed on the horizon of the steppe) was created. In Mongolian, *gher* are the round tents of nomad stockbreeders. *Yurt* is a Kazakh word. Originally, the two words designated the country of birth, the territory, dwelling place, and land, as well as the families and the herd that depended on them.

In everyday language, *gher* is now only applied to the house. If it is round, this is no doubt to resist the violent winds better. However, as photographer Patrick Bard pointed out, in a country where shamanism is very present "nothing under a gher is left to chance." Its circular framework is made up of four to ten articulated trellises, made of half branches of willow or juniper attached by a supple leather lace that enables them to be bent. The door frame is erected between two trellises, facing south—oriented, it is said, to the zodiac sign of the horse. The felt covering that protects the house, formerly made of sheep's and camels' wool and now bought ready-made, is then covered with a large white canvas, which rests on the roof poles. The poles are attached to each end of the trellises and fitted together by a crown of wood, divided into spokes, called the *toono*. This is the framework of the roof. Two posts support the weight, but they are not made of just any wood. According to ethnologist Isabelle Bianquis-Gasser, they are made of birch, a tree that once had an important role in shamanic ceremonies. Placed on each side of the hearth, they assure the connection between earth and sky. The toono's large hole lets air and sunlight pass through and is also the path of the spirits. It is protected by a felt square that is adjusted from the interior using a cord. The shadow of the sun, marked by the wooden spokes of the toono, is outlined on the walls of the gher. Previously, when the morning sun reached a very precise point on the tent canvas, it marked "small noon," time to take a welcome break. Inside the gher, the inhabitants move systematically according to the course of the sun, as indicated by the toono. The axis of the smoke that rises from the hearth represents the axis of the earth, and the toono is itself the image of the sky. Two or three can set this house up in a half hour. It weighs a little more than 440 pounds (200 kilos) and is easily loaded onto two carts. It provides 215 square feet (20 square meters) of living space. But today these technical criteria are not important. Slowly, those that protect the spirits of the steppe let the curved path of the sun enter and let the reassuring breathing of the horses be heard. These houses made of felt, wood, and cloth are disappearing, like the Mongol traditions and their way of speaking and thinking about the world.

Mongolia. The yurt is a circular construction easy to take down and transport. It is covered with felt or matting, and in humid regions, an additional layer of canvas.

Under Earth as It Is in Heaven

The collective imagination gives the subterranean, the cave, a dangerous connotation because the kingdom of the dead is found below, in dark and shadowy places. However, for some troglodytes, life underground or in hillsides is a return to the primordial cradle, Mother Earth. To hide in a cave and rest in the shelter of the original matrix, however, requires winning the favor of infernal presences through blessings and magical or religious rituals. Space, like time, must be defined, marked out, so that fertility, wealth, and longevity can be realized and can confer to the house its role of protector. Previously, the house was nothing more than a gaping hole, a devouring mouth, and women were forbidden to be present because this excavation of a house in construction, this "empty belly," contained a threat of sterility. According to the works of ethnologist Geneviève Ribaud, this is why the Beni Aissas of southern Tunisia make sure that every new excavation is done according to ancestral rites. The favorable periods to start work depend on the planets. Work can be undertaken during the first quarter of the moon, or when Jupiter or Venus appear in the sky—Venus being the morning star in the east and the evening star in west. Wednesday, the worst day, is prohibited, but Thursday, the day of Jupiter, and Friday, the day of Venus, are good days to begin. One, five, and six are beneficial numbers. One is the number for Sunday, linked to the dispenser of light—that which follows shadows and chaos. Five is the number of the center of harmony and balance. It is a lucky number for Muslims because it represents the number of daily prayers as well as the five fingers of Fātimah's hand. Finally, six is associated with Venus, and refers to the six days of divine creation. The affirmation of ethnologist Marcel Mauss that a technique is an efficient traditional act that does not differ from religion or magic is confirmed by the Beni Aissas' way of life. From the choice of a troglodytic excavation site close to relatives to the required techniques and the protective benediction of the house, the dwelling becomes the medium for memory and a way to transmit traditions.

India, Himalaya,
Zanskar region, Buddhist
monastery of Phugtal.
Troglodytic houses

Thailand. Village on
pilings on the River Kwai

Just Above the Water

Off the coast of Thailand, the Mokens of the Surin Islands, true nomads of the sea, know that the pleasure of navigating is always accompanied by the fear of sinking. But to explain the overflow of celestial downpours, they prefer to evoke the Crab, who is responsible for tides. The Crab lives under a mango tree, in the center of a pass called the "navel of the world," where freshwater and saltwater mix, where underground rivers and oceans converge with those on the surface, forming a pillar, an axis that traverses the three spheres of sky, earth, and sea. The Mokens fear this mythic place; the whirlpools caused by the Crab can swallow their boat, the *kabang*. In the past, they had been born and had died on these houseboats. They debarked upon the island to be buried there, a burial that was in contradiction to their way of life, but that signified quite well that the return into the belly of the earth could be fecund.

To build their houseboats, the Mokens scrupulously followed the ancestral know-how in order to find a type of wood that allowed them to travel, fish, and have a roof over their heads. Few species were suitable. They sometimes had to search for weeks for the type that expanded in water, ensuring that it was perfectly watertight at embarkation. Then they set up a two-section tent made of a large mat of leaves and two fork-shaped pieces of wood—one in front and the other in back—supporting a long bamboo pole. Three stones placed on the deck protected the fire and the tripod for smoking fish. According to the rhythm of their fishing, the inhabitants of this floating plant-dwelling perseveringly adjusted the rhythm of their fishing so as not to disturb the Crab, making the necessary offerings to gain his favor.

Wherever the River Flows

If the perpetual motion of the river symbolizes becoming, then its current represents the flow of time, of life and death. One must be very careful when crossing from one bank to the other. We know that the Greeks deified rivers; every year during ritual celebrations, priests sacrificed live bulls and horses to them. Human beings have always feared the caprices of rivers and the potential for floods. Whether they settle nearby on solid ground or encroach on the river's territory, inhabitants need to know how to tame the flow to keep it from taking away their houses whenever it floods.

Adapting to aquatic life requires resistant materials. In Venezuela, at the mouth of the Orenoque River, the Waroos cut piling posts from mangrove wood to build their houses. This wood does not rot and can support a surprising degree of humidity. It is also used in the Amazon region. To avoid the inundation of the world's largest river, whose waters can rise 33 or 39 feet (10 or 12 meters) during the rainy season, the inhabitants build veritable floating houses using ancestral techniques that go back to the fourteenth century.

In the extreme south of Myanmar (formerly Burma), the Inthas, or "Sons of the Lake," have

Myanmar (formerly Burma), village of Taunggyi-Aungban, on Inle Lake. The inhabitants have become masters in the art of pilings. Small gardens planted on a base of woven reeds ensure that they will have vegetables and condiments at their fingertips.

mastered the art of building on pilings. Though fish provide the main food source, the produce from their floating gardens makes a considerable contribution. These small gardens grow on a base of woven reeds, covered with silt. They need only be anchored to a long bamboo pole or attached to the pilings of the house for the inhabitants to have vegetables and condiments at their fingertips.

In Cambodia—where the mythic serpent Naga, source of life and fertility, incarnates the element of water in opposition to earth—millions of people rely on a surprising natural phenomenon: the rising of the water level of Lake Tole Sap. Swollen by the melting snow of the Himalaya and the flooding of the Mekong, this lake quadruples its surface area during the rainy season. The inhabitants have learned to adapt by building very high houses on pilings (the poorest by building houseboats). During the dry season, the people change dwellings. They move to temporary huts, erected on solid ground where cultivation is possible, and take down the floating houses.

Nigeria, Benin, lakeside village of Ganvie. Going from one house to another is done exclusively in boats.

Following pages: India, Kashmir, Srinagar. Houseboats

Abandoned Huts

It is said that the tent stakes of nomads are all pillars of the world, as if by building their own universe, nomads revisit the original creation. But what symbolic value should be given to huts—often built in haste and abandoned as soon as it's time to leave with the herd or to look for other places to hunt? According to ethnologists, the importance and the place given to *fire* could correspond to a representation of the world, to a way of taking possession of a place. The Masai in Kenya set up their camp in a circle, which they surround with a thorny hedge to protect themselves from predators. In the center, they place their riches, the sheep and oxen, which are also their purpose for living. According to a Masai proverb, "A man without a herd is not a man." Formerly, their structure was abandoned at each move, but the roof and the tanned ox hides that covered the walls were kept. This was the time of the great herds, before the drought that turned the place into a desert. Today some Masai tribes have semipermanent camps used only for sleeping, but they still use the plan for temporary camping huts. Custom dictates that each woman build and maintain her hut. She draws on the ground—without string or measuring instrument—a kind of rectangle with rounded angles. The dimensions do not vary from one place to another: the inhabitable space is 5 feet (1.5 meters) high, 3 feet (1 meter) wide, and 13 feet (4 meters) long. Flexible poles in the ground are attached in a rounded shape to a large ridgepole. This typically Masai structure supports a covering of several layers of dried grass held together by a mixture of mud and dung. The covering ends 20 inches (50 cm) above the ground to allow air circulation. The Masai enter into this one room only at night—through an animal-skin door. The fire is in the middle of the space, the men on the left and the women on the right. For the Masai, the fire symbolizes the sun, which gives heat and life. It is the eye of God, his presence among mortals. This central place for the fire, at equal distance from both sexes, shows the place of the divine in daily actions.

Kenya, Masai village.
Building the hut,
gathering cob
and branches,
is woman's work.

Fleeting Masterpiece

The huts of the Pygmies look like they are made out of plant tiles. The cone roofs of these often bamboo, often round huts in central Africa are frequently covered with leaves. The leaves are from plants in the Marantaceae family, which are found in the undergrowth of large forests. The huts are not made from a simple arrangement of branches but are complex constructions that follow a very precise know-how. Pygmy women build their houses when they are married, but bachelors are able to erect their huts themselves. The gigantic Marantaceae leaves are sometimes as big as 20 inches (50 cm). They are gathered and stacked in the same direction before being transported in a tight bundle to the next campsite, where the women, sitting on the ground, sort them out and turn them over one by one. With a machete, they cut them so that each leaf fits on a wooden stalk that, together, form the framework of the hut: a kind of skeleton of flexible and curved stems that make the vaulted trellis. The women lay down the prepared leaves a bit like a roofer lays roof tiles, each one overlapping the other. The work proceeds from the base of the hut to the summit. The outside of the leaf, which is less fragile, is turned toward the exterior. According to ethnologist Guy Phillippart, five leaves are enough to cover nearly 8 inches (20 cm). The women erect this fleeting masterpiece of leaves very quickly. It is only used for a few days and sometimes only for a night.

Leaves adorning huts in this way look like the scales on the backs of pangolins. These mammals of astonishing morphology, which eat ants and termites, are totemic in some tribes, and eating their flesh is prohibited. They probably play a role of protector.

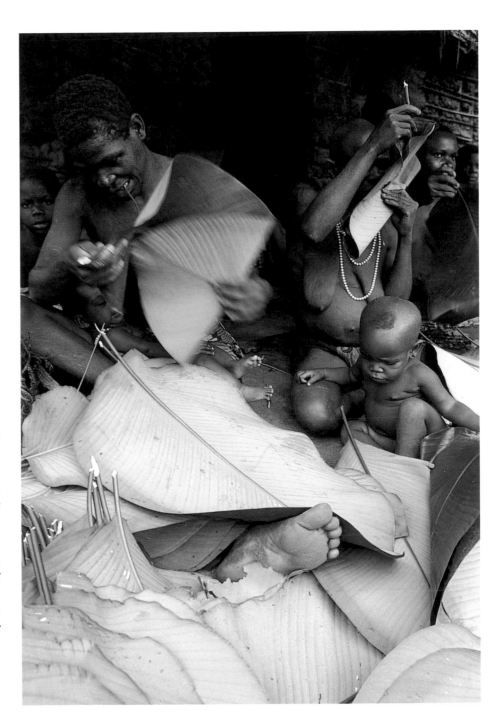

Opposite: Cameroon. Adapted to everyone's size, Pygmy huts serve mostly as shelter for the night and food storage.

Above: Congo. These Pygmy women gather large leaves that are sewn together to make the hut's covering.

Mud for Building

For millennia, humans have known how to make their dwellings rise from the earth. Whatever the form of the habitat or the region of the world—India, China, Africa, America—the use of raw earth has been mastered. Wet, dug out, piled in mounds, as filler or aggregate for a roof or to maintain a pile of leaves, the use of earth molded according to needs is omnipresent. An extract from the topsoil, this raw material has allowed the astonishing architecture of cities and villages, palaces and mosques. If the earth is sandy, rich in gravel, and without much clay, it is compacted using a pestle inside a wooden frame. It hardens as it dries in this frame.

Adobe—bricks of raw earth dried in the sun—is one of the oldest building materials. It was used in Mesopotamia as early as the third millennium BC. The Bible mentions this technique, used for palaces, temples, and walls, in recounting the construction of the Tower of Babel. It is estimated that it took 36 million bricks to make the ziggurat of Babylon. The adobe technique is still found in Morocco, Afghanistan, Peru, and Brazil. Earth, to which straw is added, is kneaded by hand, then pressed between two boards or placed in molds. The mixture, often a very claylike earth combined with all kinds of plant fibers, is applied directly onto racks of woven wood. It is also modeled into packs or logs mounted on top of each other to make compact walls. In Mali, the famous mosques of Djenné and Gao are made of adobe.

Opposite: Mauritania, Goubenwamur. Drying mud bricks in the sun

Following pages: Algeria. Mud village of the ksar of Taghit, facing the sand dunes of the Sahara

Clay and Water

In northern Togo, the Tamberma erect veritable fortresses of earth. These granaries for sorghum, millet, or corn—donjons topped with a straw cone—encircle the dwelling. Clay and water give them the status of living beings; they represent the flesh and blood of the *tata* (house). When the walls are finally dry, they are waterproofed with a coating whose base is made from the African locust tree. This gives the walls their particular color. The village architects alone are authorized to build one tata per season. Though the entire village helps—some mixing, some carrying water—only the architect is responsible for the tata. The sacred power of this mastery of earth is incarnated in the house; the entrance to the tata always faces the setting sun in homage to the sun god, who was the source of this dwelling. As for the superposed distribution of the different floors, the ground floor, symbolizing the underground world, is allotted to the ancestors; the terrace, or the terrestrial world, is for mortals; and the highest place, the roof ridge, is given to the gods. In this verticality, the sacred nature of the place, in which the various worlds are united and required to communicate, is reinforced.

Togo, Koulankou. The
tata, a Tamberma dwelling,
is a fortress built with
water and clay.

Reed Peoples

In the story of the "Three Little Pigs," the straw, wood, and brick houses sum up the art of living in a particular type of house. According to psychoanalyst Bruno Bettelheim, the story recapitulates progress in construction and shows that patience is by far the best means to secure the most reliable house.

In hot and humid countries, where temperature variation is almost nonexistent throughout the year, wood, reeds, bamboo, and plant fibers are the materials most often used for a well-ventilated house.

In Japan, despite considerable climatic differences between the northern and southern sections of the island, the subtropical model of the south is imposed throughout the entire country. The houses have elevated floors, and their wood- and mulberry-paper panels are adjusted to the season. In Côte d'Ivoire and Malaysia, inhabitants near the lagoons build lodgings whose walls of palm and bamboo not only let air circulate freely, but also filter the bright light.

Since the Sumerian Period, the Madan Arabs have chosen to live in an unusual territory of marshland located between the Tigris and Euphrates rivers. The "country between the two rivers" is said to have inspired the legend of earthly paradise, or the Garden of Eden, and not so long ago, people still went there to honor the tree of Adam. Only one building material is found in this region: a giant reed called Phragmites, from which these "people of the reeds" have built their large huts, or *mudhifs*, from floor to ceiling, using arches covered with matting. For a long time in the Middle East, Arabs and Persians had re-created the age-old methods used to build their homes, but today the tradition has all but disappeared.

Iraq. The marshlands that extended between the Tigris and Euphrates rivers, inhabited by the Madan, are almost completely dried out today.

Learning a Skill

Throughout their history, humans have developed instruments and techniques to build walls and structures of wood, clay, stone, leaf, and hide. But not everyone is allowed to build. In many cultures, women erect the hut or tent; in others, women are prohibited from participating in the work. A corps of recognized and feared builders, carpenters, and masons, who are in charge of the building and the proper rites, can be called upon. They are rarely from outside the family or tribe. In building, the potential architectural style carries meaning, as does the division of space between sexes and generations, animals, spirits, and gods. But whatever the living space, it is necessary to have specific gestures repeated and know-how transmitted from guardians of tradition, or from innovators who defy nature or create with the elements. The creation of a new living space reconstructs human history.

We know that five thousand years ago Mesopotamian masons already used measuring strings, stakes, plumb lines, mortarboards, and trowels. They drew a plan for a house on the ground and traced the right angles of a lodging using a rope with calibrated knots. To build, they used raw and coated bricks. The Mesopotamian architects built entire cities, temples, palaces, towers, domes, vaults, and stairways, pushing decoration to a surprising level of richness and aesthetics. At the same time, in the core of the Mesopotamian marshes, houses were constructed using reeds tied in sheaths. They were then set up to form an arched framework and covered with braided reeds. Two pillars framed the entrance door, and reed turrets—apparently for no reason beyond symbolic orientation—decorated two or three corners of the dwelling. If the cities of raw brick have disappeared today, the techniques used since the fourth century BC have not changed, and *mudhif*s (reed houses) still exist in Iraq.

Opposite: Northwest Greenland. Cutting out blocks of ice to build an igloo

Above: Southern Sudan, Shilluck. Wooden arches used to build huts

Russia, Tuva. Blessing of
a tent by a female shaman

The Right Day

Choosing the right day to set up their *gher* is the first concern of the Mongols, and according to the ethnologist Isabelle Bianquis-Gasser, a calendar is never used to determine the favorable moment. It is the same in China, where the homeowner's date of birth and sign in the cosmic cycle (horse, rabbit, sheep, rat, etc.) are taken into consideration before building. In North America, the Caddo Indians wait for the decision of an oracle before the "first striking of the pole" on a circle drawn in advance; each villager participates in erecting a dwelling structure, which the women then cover with thatch. It is also under favorable auspices that Hmong families build their houses with the help of neighbors. When the right moment has come, the house's owner calls for their help. According to ethnologists Paul and Elaine Lewis, when the first two pillars of the foundation have been set up, the head of the family declares, "I live here! From now on, all evil spirits will stay far away!" This is a good way to chase away the supernatural owners of the site.

In some villages of Southeast Asia, it is absolutely essential that the pillars of a house not be aligned with those of the house next to it. Such an alignment would produce a conflict between the spirits of different domiciles, which could only have negative consequences on the neighbors' relationship. The Beni Aissas of southern Tunisia want to assure that everything is done to attract good fortune. To call down a blessing upon the place, on the inhabitant, and on those who helped with the work, the head of the family sacrifices a lamb. In some places, such as Zakkar in western Algeria, three sacrifices are made: one for the foundation, one for the threshold, and one for the central pillar and the main girder. In Yun-Nan, China, protection rites consist of a sacrifice to the earth—made when the work is complete—to appease the Dragon, god of the ground and house. But when the first stone is placed, libations are offered to the patron spirit of carpenters, Lu Ban. And this is not just any stone, since it has to face the bad spirits that could disrupt construction.

A Mineral, Animal, or Plant Covering

The first person who traced the plan of a house on the ground around him- or herself drew a tiny border between the inside and the outside, the domestic and the wild space, between the human being and the spirits or ancestors. Only the enclosure of a house, like protective clothing, isolates from the exterior. Though the space remains open, letting the sun and moon pass, this constructed boundary is significant, because activities carried out in the interior and exterior are not the same. This mineral, animal-flesh, or plant cocoon, which is adjusted according to the human body, dreams, beliefs, and fears, is like a second skin. The house is personified, feminized—taking on the form of a primordial belly and cradle of life—or it echoes the cavity of the tomb. In a play of fittings and likenesses, the body of the house responds to the natural needs of the human body, accepts and ritualizes them.

Kenya, village on Turkana Lake. Straw houses

Protector of sleep and of the family hierarchy, the dwelling assigns each person his or her role and place.

In some ethnic groups, living space is divided according to age, sex, and function. In many cultures, women reign as mistresses of the kitchen, a place where the family unit often finds itself, far from feast-day splendors. The hearth has given way to the stove, but we keep in memory this mythic value of the fire that brings us together. In the past, houses were counted by the number of fires.

As for visitors waiting on the threshold, they can know whatever intimacy the hosts allow them by penetrating into the common room. There are traditions and well-guarded family secrets in these private spaces. So that no one is offended—not even the gods, who watch over the happiness and prosperity of the house—the inhabitants must know how to moderate their speech and actions. Anyone who bursts abruptly into a place will remain a stranger to the people living there, if he or she does not respect the implicit rules, because the family space forms a coherent whole. Any infraction is almost like a danger or threat. This is why the inauguration of a new construction often requires a special ceremony, in which the inhabitants of the village participate. A new building is not added without the consent of the group; it must be a part of the common traditional history. The blessings of the priests, who accompany the village chief, thus bring the feeling of belonging, and the fundamental values transmitted from ancestors, into the present. The building of a house offers the occasion to affirm a certain way of being in the world.

Thus, to parody the poets, the walls talk. The primary goal of the slow and patient work of archeologists is to learn about the people, near or faraway in time, who lived in a place. The house stands like a stela, a monument, where the longevity of the architectural techniques and forms tells us about the past.

Any house testifies to the order and mastery of materials, as precarious as those materials may be in extreme climates. It is an imprint of life that is significant in itself since it speaks about the conditions of life.

Forms of Life

When a child draws a house, the house spontaneously takes the shape of a face. It has two eyes, a nose, the door as a mouth, and the roof as a hat. It is personified, as though the place where we live must have a human face. Sacred space for some, profane for others, the house cannot ignore the imprint of the human body, of the things the body needs: to breathe, nourish itself, sleep, have sex. The importance of these basic needs, and the responses given to them, determine the way of life. Where do the inhabitants eat? When and with whom? Why at a table or seated on a floor? What place is reserved for each man, woman, or child, to sleep?

If privacy is protected, immediately the shape and orientation of the windows change. Different lifestyles influence the shapes of the habitat, the division and distribution of domestic spaces. The body moves in the space: right, left, in front of, behind, and in this way, gives a certain number of orientation indicators, like the four walls of houses that designate the four cardinal points. In some nomadic cultures, the spine is likened to the central pillar of the house, itself the image of the cosmic pillar. The roof or dome represents the skull, in relationship with the sky, and the opening left for the passage of smoke also allows spirits, gods, and shamans to pass. In India, the symbolic orifice of the crown of the head, through which the soul leaves the body at the moment of death, has the same name as that of the turret. Every society models its dwelling place according to its representation of the body, according to social proximity to other bodies, the way it fits into its environment. This is why houses in the same village look alike and are sometimes identical. Those houses indicate that the group adheres to the same representations, a unity in the fitting together of worlds: bodily, human, and cosmic. If these connections disappear, building a domicile only has a utilitarian function, and living in a landscape aims at controlling and modifying without a primary concern for balance and harmony with the environment. As for the body of the house, it no longer forms a whole or resembles a person in its singularity. For traditional societies, humankind, the house, and the universe are in symbiosis.

Nepal, Charkha village. The chimney of nomad tents is the place where the world of the house communicates with the world of the spirits.

Nepal, Charkha, Dolpo village. In the Himalaya, the inhabitants love to compare their dwelling to a woman whose beauty they venerate.

As Beautiful as the Day

"The house is a sanctuary; the lintel of the threshold is gold; the step, turquoise; the door is iron; the window bar, a conch; the beam, a ladder of agate." This is how in Tarap, Tibet, in the Himalayan valleys, the peasants chant praises to their house as if it were a woman adorned with a thousand jewels. As the New Year approaches at the winter solstice, the inhabitants get rid of the soot left by the hearth—which smokes throughout the day—as well as its stains and impurities. Like everything that lives, the house must die and be reborn. Finally, to protect it, a picture of a pig—an evil animal—that stops sickness from entering is attached to the inside of the door. In the collective unconscious the house is a person; it is decorated as well as it can be; it is respected because it has been the house of one's ancestors and sometimes the witness of long genealogies. It is fashioned in the inhabitants' image, modifying, adding, or eliminating some rooms. This inscription in the walls of lineages, together with events in the family and social history, is valuable to the collective memory. The abandoned house tumbles into oblivion. It marks the disappearance of its occupants as well as its own demise. It prefigures death, like a body in decomposition, like a symbolic return to chaos.

In all cultures, the living space, for both sedentary peoples and nomads, is material and symbolic wealth. Its different stages of construction, its annual cleaning, and its maintenance repairs are accompanied by magical or religious rituals. Blessings, libations, and offerings are made to the gods as well as to the house itself, because it is up to the house to watch over the good life of mortals, ensure their protection when they give themselves up to sleep. For this reason, the Lao of Southeast Asia prefer to sleep lying in a direction perpendicular to the line of the roof ridge. To lie parallel to that line would bring bad luck, because this is the position reserved for the dead. In Madagascar, the layout of the house also presides over one's destiny, according to the orientation of people and objects, such as an ancestor corner, bed, large jug, place of the rich and place of the poor. It assigns to each inhabitant his or her position, and this order cannot be upset without the risk of disturbing someone's fate.

Body of Ice

The Inuit of the Arctic know how to fulfill the imperative of having a cozy house when it is −58°F (−50°C) outside. In times past, they lived through winter in half-buried houses, with low walls of stone and peat. They entered through the roof, made of and covered by whale bones. Dried seal bladders were arranged around openings to let the rare light in. But when they moved for the big hunts, the Inuit built an igloo that would melt in the spring. In this way, real villages were organized by family.

For the Inuit, an invisible line unites the universe, the human body, and the house. The universe itself is a house, and the body, an igloo. Moreover, according to Michel Therrien, the same terms designate the various parts of the house and of the human body. *Pharynx* designates the access hall of the igloo, a small tunnel that stops the glacial wind from penetrating. One use of the word involves the passage of food, the other, the passage of men, women, and children, as well as game captured for consumption. The orifice arranged at the back of the igloo to evacuate excrement and garbage is called the *anus*. Through this hole, the sick and dead pass—as if passing through the opening of the living, the *vulva*, were impossible. The *nose* represents the aeration hole of the dwelling. The *eardrum* is the window. As a whole, the igloo represents the body of a pregnant woman. The assimilation is so compelling that a pregnant woman oversees her husband carefully cutting the last block of packed snow; it is used as the keystone of the arch of the igloo's dome. It must be placed perpendicular to the axis of the door so that the child will be in this position at the time of birth, to make the birth easier. It is understandable that the thaw of this house of snow is compared to menstruation. The term that designates the uterus is the equivalent of the "small platform," the part of the igloo covered with animal skins and used as a seat or bed. It allows the fire, set down on a tripod of reindeer bones, to be watched over. The feminine form of round dwellings is a return to the maternal womb and intrauterine life. Some Inuit legends evoke the memories of a hero from a time when he lived in a warm, comfortable house reminiscent of his fetal life. Thus, as the elders believe, life is everything, and everything is life.

Opposite: Canada. Each room of the traditional Inuit house corresponds to a part of the human body.

Above: Northwestern Greenland. Construction of an igloo, a souvenir of fetal life, according to Inuit legend

Attention: Dangerous Cocoon

To make your house a place that really belongs to you is a Western attempt to make the home a place to withdraw. The dwelling protects against more than insects, wildcats, night, or inclement weather; it protects against a diffused feeling of aggression. A small space is enough to make a patiently woven cocoon, a second skin into which you can slide to learn all that the word *interior* signifies. Thus, the walls mark out a private space. The extended family, the community, does not always share the space, which is constructed to restore the inhabitants, even transform them once the door is closed. No doubt with the progress of household appliances and the massive construction of lodgings, the significance of the house has changed—as has that of the neighborhood—and the tradition of collective building has disappeared. But since it involves covering oneself with bricks or cement blocks, wood and glass, and curling up in the innermost recesses of a dwelling, what one puts there of oneself makes up the house's essential attraction.

On the high plateau of the southern Andes in Argentina, this idea of a cocoon lodging seems very surprising. The *casa del campo*, an adobe house made of earth, straw, and water—with a roof of branches—is used in the pasture areas far from the village. Referring to this house of tiny windows, a dirt floor, and only one main room, the ancient ones say that you have to kill it so that it will not eat you. Like an infernal mouth always hungry, it is such a devourer that once built, it has to be pierced with arrows during a strange celebration called the *Flechada*, or arrow celebration. Ethnologist Lucilla Bulgado reports that this is a protection rite. Eggs, suspended from the ceiling by red wool strings, are pierced by small arrows. The egg white and yolk fall into a hole dug in the floor, as an offering to the earth. Like the house, the earth has a soul and the fear of being gobbled is ever present during construction. Once the spirit of the house has been killed, it has to be fed constantly. When a cow is slaughtered, blood is offered in the form of a cross drawn on the outside walls. If the house is given this vital energy, why would it return for that of the occupants?

Tunisia. A dugout—an underground house—with its central patio

A Well from the Sky

An opening in the center of a roof facilitates communication between the world above and the underworld, the ascending and descending movements of the hearth spirits, shamans, and souls. Besides its symbolic signification, this improvised chimney has a more prosaic function: it evacuates the smoke from the central fire, which is located just below it. It can also act as a window through which the sunlight passes—often the only source of light in the room. In the past, in some poor houses in the Chinese countryside, a fixed skylight was made using transparent tiles. It was called the "artificial sky"; "the artificial earth" referred to the boards used to set the boundaries of interior space. When dwellings are so close together that terraces are used as streets, this hole in the roof is often the only way to enter a house, via a ladder made from a notched trunk. The hole lets the rainwater come through and fall into a kind of collector in the middle of the room or simply into a hole dug into the dirt floor. In Siberia, China, Mongolia, Tibet, and Sudan, this same opening, called the "sky window," is found. Fire, light, water: the sacred characteristics of the fire and the water that fights it explain the central position of the opening, at the summit of the dwelling. This natural chimney, which serves as stovepipe duct and aeration inlet, has a disadvantage:

Siberia. Interior of a Nenet
tent. The chimney also
functions as a window.

it does not completely evacuate the smoke. For a Western heating specialist, building a chimney with insufficient draw would be the worst shame. But ambient smoke is not here thought of as harmful because it keeps insects away, hardens the ridgepole with its black tar coating, and smokes meat. A few years ago, a Western traveler returning from a village in Nepal recounted that you could only enter the living room from the ground floor, which was reserved for animals, via a ladder. The common room was very smoky but there was no sense in opening a window, which was small anyway, to let the freezing air in. Between the posts, on tightened strings, were pieces of sheep's meat oozing grease. A few drops sometimes fell on the sleepers at night, but everyone was gathered together near the fire of the stone hearth, and the essential thing was to keep warm.

The nomad hunters of central Africa also keep a fire in their huts to smoke game, which preserves it for several days, despite the muggy heat. But there is no aeration hole. Here again the constant smoke, which chases away mosquitoes and other insects, leaves tar on the roof of the shelter that makes it watertight. And you can see in the clearing of a tropical forest houses breathing through all their plant pores.

Mongolia. In the house, smoke fireproofs the wooden beams and keeps insects away.

Construction Game

Who erects the hut or tent, lays down the bricks, or cuts the poles? It is very often the woman. A woman erects the *lobembe* of Pygmy couples, the huts of the Masai in Kenya, and those of the Bushmen in the Kalahari. Women prepare the skin-covered tents of the Samoyeds in Siberia and of the various tribes living on the tundra. Setting up and taking down these temporary dwellings, folding them up, putting them away, and getting them ready to be transported seems to be a task handed down to women, as if it is incumbent upon them to make the fragility of the shelter maternal and pro-

tective. In the Hoggar Desert, before putting up a tent, men and women drawn a line on the ground. Then the women dig the twenty holes for the stakes, which the men put up. They dig using a particular knife for keeping away the evil eye and the jinn. The men put up the lateral and central stakes next. A canopy of narrow black bands, woven from goat hairs and sewn together, covers these posts. But the women must not help with this stage of construction.

In Zanskar and Ladakh, custom prescribes that the patriarch give the large family house and its

Kenya. The Turkana set up a hut. Only the women, who are devoted to the house, know how to do it quickly.

property to the oldest son when he marries. The patriarch then lives in a small house, whose construction he must supervise, with the women and children. The family makes the adobe bricks, with cousins and friends actively participating. Mutual aid is also enlisted by the Karen, Lahu, and Akhas of Thailand. Gender is irrelevant; everyone contributes to the cutting of wood and the gathering of materials in the nearby forest according to his or her strength and skills. For the occasion, the owner kills a pig and organizes a celebration. Later, it will be up to the owner and his family to help with a new construction. No one ever thinks of breaking this rule of solidarity. On the other hand, this is no longer practiced by the Emerillons of Guyana. Though building remains the work of men, the community no longer participates, beyond a brother or brother-in-law. What is at stake is neither solidarity nor reciprocity, but rather personal prestige. By building his house alone, a man proves his valor and skill to the community, even if he is aided by the chainsaws and motors that have begun to replace ancient traditions.

Niger. A tent of goat and camel skin is set up on its wooden supports.

United States. A
Cree tent. For many
nomadic peoples, fire
has a sacred dimension.

Light the Fire

When was the first lamp illuminated? Though historians cannot pinpoint the date, in an essay dedicated to the night, writer Tang Ke Yang remembers a time not so long ago in China, before electricity was brought to the countryside, when you had to watch over the lamp oil—a very expensive commodity. Light was the privilege of well-to-do families. For centuries, entire populations marveled at the glowing of fireflies or worms, the light of the moon, and the sparkling of the stars. This is probably why many legends recount the origin of the Milky Way and that of the patterns of the moon, sometimes inhabited by a hare, sometimes by a toad. In many cultures, the glow of fire was surrounded by taboos, which sometimes curbed its use. It was often deified, as it was in China, where it was called *Yen-ti*. Under penalty of attracting divine thunderbolts, stepping over the hearth of the house was prohibited.

In Japan, the god of the stove was more important: the stove's fire, of which the dwelling was guardian, was only put out if someone in the family died. Great consideration was also given to other divinities that guarded the vital elements. In addition to luck, Ebisu and Daikoku represented wells and toilets. Their role was to guarantee the purity of these premises.

In Mongolia, fire symbolizes the family and its lineage. The role of the woman is to keep it going. During the marriage ceremony, a father transmits to his son a little of his own fire to start his family. Walking on the hearth, bumping into it, letting the fire go out deliberately, or throwing impure things in it can be seen as a provocation. At the New Year, the fire spirit is revived with offerings of meat—particularly pieces of sheep's snout—and libations of alcohol. This custom is called "giving the first mouthful to the fire." According to the Mongol conception, by giving homage to the fire in the center of the *gher*, participants in this celebration venerate, by analogy, the center of the world.

Nepal, Mustang.
Demon traps at the
house entrance

Plain or with Butter

Founding a house requires as precise a ceremony as founding a city or village. Even if all the favorable conditions are met, no step, from the laying of the first stone to the laying of the last, should be skipped—just as none of the rites of passage that extend from birth to death should be forgotten. In Tibet, once the door frame has been put up, small pieces of cloth in beneficial colors—corresponding to the five cosmic elements and the organs of the body—are nailed on the upper part of the frame. Next, the owner spreads grains of barley in the lower corners of the frame so that health and prosperity enter through this door. Finally, he applies a little butter from the female yak so that sickness spares men and their herds. Grilled barley flour, butter, milk, and tea are the basic foods of Tibet. The nomads, sedentary in winter, begin the day by offering milk to the terrestrial and celestial spirits. Butter, which lights the small lamps placed on the family altar as offerings to the gods, probably has the same function. However, since the house is identified with the body, putting a piece of butter on the lintel of the door or on the mats of the tent, also goes back to the prescriptions of traditional Tibetan medicine: butter increases heat, force, and longevity. The house is symbolically nourished, as one's body is nourished, to guarantee that the stomach—representing the granary or the storerooms—receives good harvests. The same rite is performed for the window frames. Throughout construction, three stones rest one on top of the other on the roof frame. They bar the route for demons and evil spirits, which could occupy the space even before the owners move in. Doors, windows, and aeration holes in the roof: these orifices are dangerous because no one knows how unhappiness penetrates into a house or sickness into the body. At the entrance, religious formulas, protective objects—sometimes stuffed goat heads—playact as exorcists. When the house is finished, another ceremony consecrates it.

Nepal, Mustang. The doorstep is heavily protected from evil spirits with the use of talismans.

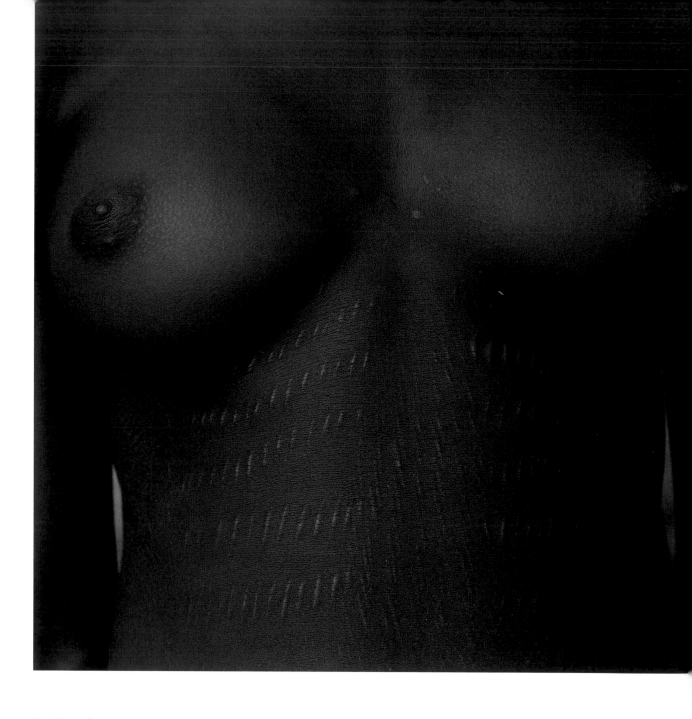

Mother House

This mineral, animal, or vegetable covering that a human draws around his or her own flesh, called a house, is a great matrix. It is the protective and nourishing mother, the place where the outside harvest—meager or abundant—is transformed into flour, pancakes, bread; a place where milk and fruits are kept. If the first human boundary, a mother's womb, is recorded in the unconscious from the time of conception, it must be left behind to come into the world and into life. This passage through the narrow door of birth gives

rise to many others, celebrated in myths and religious ceremonies as an access to a new state, a symbolic way of being reborn. The walls of the house are the first special boundaries of the physical body.

The cost of building materials and their abundance or rarity are only partly responsible for the structures adopted. In northern Togo, when the Tamberma people make their habitat into a replica of the human body, they do so from a deep desire for symbiosis with the earth—and because

Togo, Tamberma country. Torso of a young Tamberma woman bearing ethnic scarifications

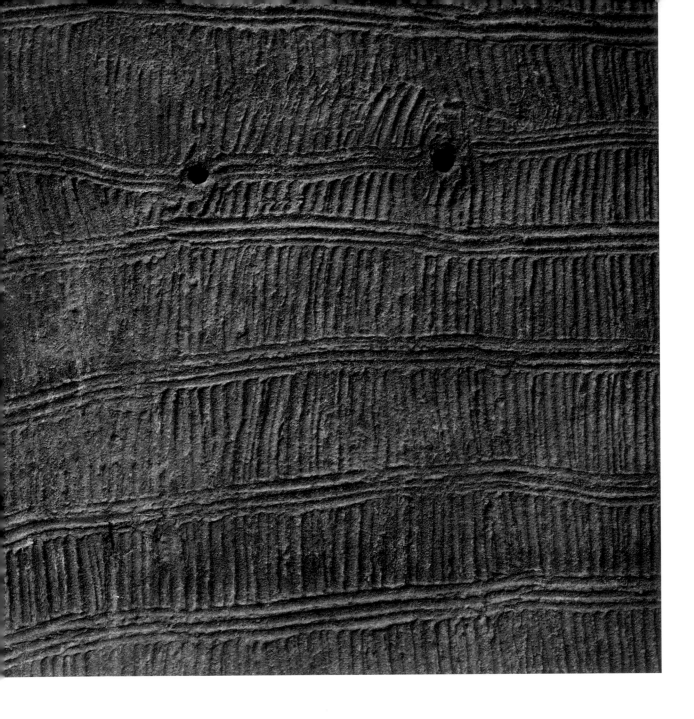

a transference of the original mother to the house takes place. It is a realistic way to answer the question, Where do we come from? We come from an original mother whose representation can be modeled explicitly from the earth. Like the universal father, Adam (*adama* in Hebrew)—created, according to the Bible, by a divine breath from the land—and like the mother of all living, the archaic mother goddess, Eve, the traditional house, the *tata*, exists to set into architecture a human origin that would otherwise be inconceivable. This is why,

in this representation, the mother house possesses all that is necessary to live. Its construction is conceived like a birth. The clay and water used for fabrication is symbolically transformed into flesh and blood. The small orifices of the facade are two eyes; the door is a mouth; the lintel, a tongue. The millstones that grind the grain are teeth. Scarifications drawn on the walls of buildings recapture the face and body of woman, and these imprints in the flesh of the house bestow on it the identification signs of its inhabitants.

Togo, Tamberma country. Drawings on the wall in the image of the human body

A Grave Before Its Time

The poet Jean Tardieu wonders, "Since there is a wall, what happens behind it?" More than simple boundaries, walls mark the enclosure, offering a pretext to intimacy tinged with virtue and morals. Family secrets, abuse, or exclusion are not exposed to daylight any more than wealth or poverty. Walls are also signs of power and authority. The house is no longer a cradle, but is more like a tomb. Even so, the Dogon in Mali do not hesitate to sleep in the position that they will have in their graves. The man is on the right, facing the west, the woman, on the left, facing the east, in a kind of general rehearsal before eternity.

Perhaps the idea of finishing one's days in the grave does not frighten some, but the dark side of dwellings was once particularly feared in Asia, where protector fetishes were often employed. In Japan, a stone was placed in a high spot to keep away harmful influences. The Berbers in Morocco called the wall with the door "the wall of darkness" or "the grave." A saying recounted by sociologist Pierre Bourdieu sums up the function attributed to each wall, according to its shade or light: "When a boy is born, the walls of light rejoice; when a dead person leaves the house, the dark walls cry." The expression "to hold a wall" meant that a person was sick. It was also used to express that a person was not seated at the place of honor, before the loom, but relegated to a dark part of the house. In an essay about the cultural perception of space, anthropologist Edward T. Hall notes that Arabs often use the word *tomb* to designate closed spaces, because they find it unbearable to be closed in by walls. Being crammed into interior spaces seems to bother them, while being outside, in a souk, for example, among the effects of a crowd where people are pressed together, does not frighten them. Therefore, their ideal house must meet several criteria: a high ceiling that does not obstruct the visual field, a large space, and an open view. When a neighbor blocks this view by building a house or a wall, which is unfortunately inevitable in a city, it is interpreted as a contemptuous act.

On the other hand, interior crowding does not bother the Japanese, who are willing to sleep on the floor very close to each other if necessary. Moreover, it is said that the word *privacy* does not exist in their language, though escaping the indiscrete looks from the exterior seems to be a preoccupation. If closeness to the other is not disturbing, to live in an attached house and have to share a wall is detestable, above all in an apartment. But what is unbearable for the Masai of Kenya is the very idea of a house. To have a hut over your head already represents the beginning of confinement.

Mauritania. Decorations in a bedroom. The hot climate encourages families to withdraw into the interior of their houses.

Master Craftsmen

About twenty-five hundred years ago, the Chaldeans already knew how to make the scaffolding used to build their monuments. As for carpenters, you can go back to the Flood and Noah's ark: they are as old as the world. According to the Bible, the carpenters of the Temple of Solomon went in different directions after their work was finished, to propagate their know-how throughout the earth. In the West, these individuals have always enjoyed a special status among artisans because they were indispensable for the great works of cathedrals, castles, and cities, and even simple half-timber farms. On the feast day of Saint Joseph, the patron saint of carpenters, the journeymen promenaded their masterpieces through the streets, a form of advertising ahead of its time that enabled people to admire the skill and talent of each carpenter in the great complexity of these works. Not just anyone could be a carpenter. In the past, gaining a carpenter's good graces in China was an absolute priority because he had to hang a mirror from the ridgepole to chase away evil spirits—an indispensable action before the house could be inhabited. Likewise, no one forgot to offer libations to the spirit of carpenters, guarantor of the building. In Japan, when a house was completed, the master carpenter was accompanied home with great pomp. The opulence of the procession showed the fortune of the future occupants and the artisan.

China, Guizhou-Guangxi
Province, Gaocheng,
village of the Dong
minority. The carpenter–
architects are considered
great masters.

Formerly the carpenter was both master crafts-man and mason. In villages, out of concern for economy or because of solidarity among neighbors, the owners dug the foundations themselves, cut the trees, and even did the roofing. The carpenter drew up the plan and directed the work. A real architect, the carpenter designed the entire project, chose the location of the pillars, and even the shape of the roof. Like the medieval artisans of the West, the carpenters organized into guilds and joined similar interests—in this case belonging to a Buddhist or Shintoist temple, a castle, or an emperor's court. This was not only a way to have a qualified workforce nearby but also a good way to form a real power, because they were faithful to the authority to which they belonged. In this way, the masters transmitted building manuals, where the secrets of the profession were found from generation to generation. For example, the carpenters knew how to make incredible floors for the rich aristocrats. At night the *kamis*, Japanese spirits of nature, or thieves, loved to get into houses. The floor would vibrate with a melodic scale, warning the sleeping owner of the importune visit. Referring to the birds that sing at twilight, the carpenters called this the "nightingale floor." In the sixteenth century, the political authorities ended up fearing the carpenters and the corporations were dissolved.

Ecuador. Construction of a communal house in the Amazon forest

Forbidden Zone

The inhabitable space, even when reduced to a large common room, is divided according to very precise rules among the husband, the wife or wives, children, distinguished guests, and strangers passing through. The internal organization of the house differs greatly from one culture to the next, but commonly a space is reserved for each activity: cooking, eating, resting, sleeping, receiving guests, washing, etc. This division seems banal today in the West. However, these rooms did not have a determined function until the eighteenth century. Beds and tables changed places according to mood, clarifying the origin of the expression "to put up a table." In China, chairs could not be moved without the authorization of the host. According to anthropologist Edward T. Hall, this would be equivalent to moving a partition or screen.

On the island of Tanebar-Evav, in the Kei archipelago, Indonesia, it is a bad omen to hit the *totoma*, a large post protruding from the floor that gives rhythm to the space. The totoma concretely sets the boundary of the area reserved for guests close to the entrance, and that reserved for the master of the house on the hearth side. Under the Mongol *gher*, tradition previously regulated the disposition of people. To the right was the area allotted to women, to the left, the area given to men, and at the back was the place of honor—with sacred objects that have been dethroned today by transistors. When the Berber houses of the Beni Ouarains of Morocco had two distinct rooms, one was for the men's meals, guests, and people passing through and the other was for women and children. No male visitor could penetrate there without the agreement of the head of the family. In Southeast Asia, for the Laos Isans, the most eastwardly room is given to the founder of the house, his wife, and very young children. After the couple's death, no one will sleep in this room anymore. It will be used to receive honorable guests like influential people and elders. The west room, in the direction of death, is to be used by a couple including a married son or daughter, or by pubescent girls.

Left: India, Himalaya, Zanskar. Stairways or ladders often separate private from common space.

Opposite: China, houses of the Hakkas. Interior courtyards and common kitchens on the ground floor of communal houses

Restless Sleep

According to Hindu tradition, Brahma, with his measuring stick and his hatchet, was the great architect of the universe and author of a building treatise. In India, it was necessary to respect the precepts in every house. The first precept was to avoid all impurity in daily actions. Thus the Brahmans, members of the priestly caste, purified the place where they would sleep with dried cow dung. Mountains, cemeteries, the shade of trees, tilled earth, and gurus' houses are places not very favorable for sleep. In addition, sleeping with wet feet or under the transverse beam of a house was not recommended. In traditional China, it was also better to avoid certain sleeping positions. The husband and wife never slept with their heads to the south, since this was the position of the dead in the underworld. According to French hygienists of the nineteenth century, to have good dreams, one should sleep with the head to the north, in the direction of the "flow of magnetic currents." It is also said that the north-south position of the body favors the conception of boys. On the other hand, this position is prescribed in England, where it is thought to increase life expectancy. In many other cultures, following the direction of the sun's course, east-west, is recommended. The Japanese are said to always sleep with their heads to the east, for long life.

There is always a risk involved in sleeping, in abandoning oneself to the little death. There are many rituals to ensure serene sleep and fight against nocturnal anguish, the fear of shadows and vulnerability. In the West, a person may look under his or her bed to check that the devil isn't there. Some mountain people of Vietnam have resolved the problem of visible and invisible enemies—who previously could worm their way under the houses built on stilts—by putting the houses directly on the ground. A very long time ago, as the old sages recount, the members of rival tribes slipped into the sleeping village and, sliding under the woven floor, felt their way to the warm spot made by the body of a sleeping person. Then they would pierce the sleeper with a quick stab of a dagger. After several attacks of this type, the villagers decided to eliminate the pillars under their houses.

"The head fears the feet, the feet fear the head." According to this saying of the Laos Isans of Southeast Asia, you should never sleep head-to-foot—with the exception of the elderly, whose feet can be directed toward the head of a child. The "soul post" and the "first post," respectively symbolizing the head and the feet, indicate the positions of sleeping inhabitants. The tradition of submission and authority requires that the wife's head be lower than that of her husband. Since the head is the most important part of the body for the Laos Isans, you must not step over a sleeping person and certainly must not pass over the top of his or her head.

Northern Cameroon.
Bench made of earth.
Depending on one's be-
liefs, the head or feet must
be oriented in a particular
direction during sleep.

Sweet Dreams

In India, the bed, a wood frame set on four legs, is indispensable. On top of the wood frame is a frame of solid cotton, or of ropes that can be tightened when they become loose. No sheets are used and, depending on the season, a piece of cotton or wool is used for a blanket. A person sleeps completely dressed, taking care to cover oneself from head to foot and to protect the face to avoid making any contact that could dirty oneself. A prohibition dictates that sex, birth, and death must never take place on the bed, but in the beneficial contact with the ground. When it is too hot, the men have the habit of moving their beds to sleep outside.

In Africa, they have something better than the Western pillow: a small headrest sculpted from wood. It is said that this object makes it unnecessary for stylish women to undo the sophisticated architecture of their hair styles that sometimes takes several hours of preparation—though men also use this neck protector. In reality, the head must not be in contact with the earth because it contains everyone's thoughts and identities. For the Bambara of Mali, men grow from their heads like a plant, by the "bud of the head." The head must be taken care of to remain prosperous and in good health. Some headrests are decorated with protective patterns.

In North Africa, mattresses are a piece of furniture that can be folded up. They are stacked during the day to serve as seats. As for the Japanese futon, it is unfolded in the evening on the tatami. At the end of the Middle Ages, they were hidden in cupboards, to free space. Before the intrusion of the pillow, the Japanese preferred a small neck rest made of basketwork stuffed with horsehair. Today, a very firm pillow, a kind of bag of sand, is used.

Polynesia. Siesta time for the Samoans, under the mosquito net of the large common bed

On Earth

Matting, boards, rugs, animal skins, coconut fibers, scatterings of leaves—a bed with a mattress and box spring is a luxury for many ethnicities. Because of lack of space, lack of means, and lack of necessity, ancestral habits of sleeping in comfortable conditions are not something shared throughout the world. When the Pygmies of central Africa move from camp to camp following game, they need only a fire starter, amulets for the hunt, and some baskets. After putting up their huts, the women rake the ground and spread a mattress of fresh leaves, which is covered with a mat, onto each person's place. It is framed with a barrier of logs to prevent getting too close to the fire, which burns throughout the night.

A bench—made of ice in the Antarctic and of clay in some African villages—covered with reindeer, buffalo, or zebra skin, can also be used for sleeping. However, one often makes do with a mat, which is easily transported. The Cherokee of North America long ago gave up their sleeping skins, beds, and box springs—made of woven rush turned up at each end so they could sleep head-to-foot in the tepee. Carpet pieces or synthetic blankets do the job, even though they have neither the comfort nor the aesthetics of former times. In Amazonia, nothing is better than a hammock, hung at heights that vary according to age and sex and from the ridgepole of the *carbet*—a wall-less house of bamboo posts and a roof made of palms. The women sleep closest to the ground, with which they have an affinity, the earth being fertile for all living things.

Pakistan. This elderly
Afghan refugee brought
one of his most useful
pieces of furniture,
a bench-bed, which is
easy to disassemble.

Central Heating

"Men of fire" is what the Pygmy men of central Africa call themselves, fire being so indispensable to them in the dark and humid equatorial forest. Their campsites have certain requirements: large trees to protect against rain, and a slightly open clearing. They have to be close to a creek for water, and near a large hunting territory. When these conditions are met, *lobembe*, huts from plant material, are made to serve as shelters until the next move. In spite of their ancestral knowledge of the forest, the Pygmies fear its dangers and fear, above all, the elephant, possessed by spirits. They count on the power of fire to keep it away—and all evil spirits along with it. For this reason the fire is never extinguished. The Pygmies keep a firebrand that is transported and rekindled as soon as they are settled in each new camp. In a lobembe belonging to unmarried men, the number of fires varies according to the number of bachelors. There is one fire for every two beds and one on the side of the hut. In a lobembe belonging to a couple, the fire is located at the back, where a small opening has been made. This continuously maintained fire protects the leaf-covered roof from humidity, while the smoke deposits combustion tar, consolidating the roof and making it waterproof. These tarred leaves can even be reused for the construction of a new lobembe. The constant heat and smoke also allow hunting nets and baskets to be dried, hung on one of the pegs of the roof. Over the fire, Pygmies often set up a kiln, to smoke and preserve game. The smoke also protects the food from flies.

On the other side of the world, in Siberia, in the bark tents of the Ostiaks, fire is the subject of many taboos. Despite the extreme cold, and even though it occupies a central place and heats the pot, the fire is put out at night. Beliefs take precedence here over comfort. Fire, considered to be the carrier of the family's spirit, cannot burn while the members of a family are sleeping and are, in a way, absent from their bodies. When they wake up, the spirit of the fire will be rekindled.

Central African Republic. In the middle of the forest, the fire is the secret to survival for the Pygmies.

The Kitchen

The kitchen is a very private place—almost holy—in northern India. It is a domain reserved for family members and women, who are excluded during menstruation. The domestic divinities have their appointed place here. The choice of foods being of capital importance, it is the object of strict rules within the different castes. Any intrusion, even a look, could be considered a taint. In southern India, the kitchen is no longer encircled with religiosity, but it must be located in the southeast part of the house, in the "direction of Agni," the god of fire.

In the Himalayan valleys, the common rooms are the kitchen and the dormitory. The hearth, three large stones on a metallic tripod, marks the boundary between men's and women's spaces. At winter's end, shepherds climb with their flock of sheep and yaks to high-altitude pastures, where they set up yak-hair tents. When a woman lights the fire there for the first time, she covers the three stones with butter and offers a juniper branch to the god of the hearth.

In many latitudes, cooking is done outside or under a small shelter, sometimes in an inner courtyard protected from the wind and from indiscreet looks. Though the hearth is the central element in many houses, in the Miens' houses in Thailand there are two. One is used to cook the family's food and to receive visitors, who gather around it; the other is used to keep a large earthen pot for pig food. It is prohibited for a person to sit with their back to the hearth, because the spirits that inhabit it could take offense. For the same reason, the fire is never put out, even at night.

In the apartments built by the political regime in Ulan Bator, Mongolia, modern comforts facilitate generally improved living conditions. However, on New Year's Day the women miss the kitchen under the *gher*. How can you cook a sheep on a gas stove? City women have a good pretext to meet the women of the steppe again when they need to prepare typical dishes. Nothing is better than a real fire, with enough heat and large pots, to renew the links to tradition.

Many cultures of the world seem to agree on one point: allocate women to the kitchen. For the Korowais, who live in huts built in trees, each sex has its reserved space. An exception that proves the rules, the group of men have their own hut. However, to find this example of autonomy, you have to go to New Guinea!

Opposite: Indonesia, Maluku archipelago. A Mafuru woman prepares a meal in a shelter outside the house.

Following pages: Mongolia. Woman cooking in her *gher*

Pots and Pans in Good Order

Order could seem like a household obsession, a way of organizing things to avoid the return of primordial chaos, of confusion and vagueness. It is also a way of setting up the boundaries of one's territory, appropriating one's domain with a completely personal conception of space—to which other family members must submit. The mistress of the house decides where objects go. In spite of this right, which some women burdened with domestic tasks could do without, the problem of arranging things must be resolved. In some traditional dwellings, furniture is reduced to the strictly necessary: attached shelves (rather than a wardrobe), a few chests (for clothing and precious goods), and a small piece of furniture for prayer books and jewelry. In Zankhar, one of the valleys of the Himalaya, the inhabitants often sit on the dirt floor or on a simple sheep- or yak-skin rug or blanket. Small, low tables let them set down their bowls during meals. Everything used in the kitchen—utensils, butter churn, teapot, and fuel reserve—is arranged within the women's reach. In northern Africa and the Middle East, nomads make long journeys using sculpted chests or woven and decorated bags that they load on their horses or camels. At each campsite, once the tent is set up, the women lay out in their space (to the right) mats, bedding, baby hammocks, and necessities for weaving. To the left, on the other side of the dividing curtain, the men keep the saddles, packsaddles, and decorated leather objects—exterior signs of wealth.

Yemen. Objects are exhibited as a sign of wealth.

Well Organized

Sometimes ingenious storage solutions must be found to overcome difficulties such as ambient humidity and lack of space. The Inuit build a solid wooden framework to hang and dry their clothes under the oil lamp, out of contact with the ground, where the humidity from perspiration freezes. The nomadic peoples of Congo have the same technique, hanging hunting nets and baskets from the dome of the hut or on an inside pole. Chests, iron canteens, and sticks suspended from roof joists are used for storing clothes and bedding in India. Kitchen utensils, offered as marriage gifts, are often bulkier than the furniture. A copper plate to mix pancake flour, a wooden rolling pin, and a *pata* (a small board with legs) to flatten the mixture are in-dispensable. (The pata is also used in some religious celebrations: the Indians put little statues of the divinities on it for worshipping.) Containers, copper pots used for boiling water, and the iron plate put on the hearth to cook pancakes complete the kitchen utensils (along with earthenware, copper or brass jars, and water jugs).

In West Africa, the women's possessions include *canaris* (earthenware jars that are closed with a leaf to steam-cook food), along with gourds, baskets, multicolored enamel dishes, and plastic bowls—which are sold at the market and imported from China. An abundant range of utensils, dishes, and pots show everyone that the family is prosperous and the woman sensible.

Opposite: Morocco.
Lack of space requires
the precise arrangement
of diverse objects.

Following pages: Russia,
Lamal, houses of the Kune
animal breeders. The
chimney separates the
space into distinct parts.

Family Stocks

The necessity of storing what is needed to survive during extreme weather conditions has given a maternal shape to the granaries of African villages. Under their millet-branch roofs, they look like towers or small protuberances adjoining the house. In Mali, the doors of the Dogon granaries are often sculpted with animal protectors and their locks with signs of fertility. But where do they keep the stores, inside or out, hidden or in plain view? How can they keep them from thieves and predators while showing the family's wealth? In Nepal, firewood is stored for winter on the terraced roofs. Thus, it reinforces the house's insulation. A notched post provides access if there are no stairs. In Korea, traditional kimchi pots—a real national emblem—are stored through winter by being buried in the garden. The row of pots testifies to the owners' affluence. Some Koreans affirm that there is as much kimchi as there are families, since everyone is so attached to the fabrication secrets of his or her lineage. This national specialty is not about to be dethroned by modernity. Each beginning of winter marks the period of the *Kimjang*, when brine cabbage is fermented with red peppers and garlic. In Seoul, where the traditional houses—along with the gardens—have all but disappeared architects had to really use their imaginations to take tradition into account. The kimchi pots are now kept on a small balcony designed for this purpose, and when walking through the city you can smell cabbage everywhere.

For the Beni Aissas of southern Tunisia, the storage room—which is also the main room of their troglodytic houses—plays an essential role in the community's perception of the family. The primary concern in this room is avoiding sterility, which is considered by the entire society to be supreme poverty. Social pressure is so strong that the first wealth exposed to the eyes of everyone are the children, the family's honor, the line's vitality, and a sign of prosperity. Therefore, the first part of the storeroom should be bright, in the image of the family's wealth. The second, darker part contains the jars, fitted into niches, where the food supplies are stored: olive oil, dates, lentils, dried fish, and semolina or wheat flour. The jars must number seven per row—the number of fertility and prosperity—and the position of the rows must not change. But several rows can be aligned. Following a symbolic transposition, conscious or unconscious, the woman digs a cavity in which the man buries the jars, which he has inherited from his father. The desire to attract wealth is so strong that no one must stand in front of the storeroom door. Prosperity must be allowed to enter at any time of the day or night.

Opposite: Niger. Crushing of millet in front of the house's granaries

Following pages: Mali, Dogon country. A kitchen courtyard with its pots and pans

Shell or Fortress

"Let the immortal scorpion defend my house and its descendents until the end of time!" Why not engrave this injunction in the hardwood door as a sign of protection and fertility? Let misfortune go elsewhere. Preserved in this way, the dwelling stands up against evil, famine, and sickness. The door accepts its role of guardian of the passage between the outer and the inner. It enables the inhabitants to be protected against the risks encountered outside the walls of the house. It decides in this subtle game of opening and closing whether or not to unveil its privacy. It hides from the eyes of others what must not be seen—either out of modesty or fear. The interior space is wound around a cosmic axis: a post, girder, support wall, or mat, represented in the family by the figure of the patriarch—who is in turn symbolized by the tree of life. It is the anchoring point, the entrenchment of the his-

Mali, Dogon country, Bandiagara cliff, Youga Dogourou. The houses are protected by a fortified wall.

tory of generations and of the house. The family honor and the traditions of hospitality are staged, almost dramatized, because the place in itself materializes secular rites and the story of life. Jealously watchful of its perspectives, pierced into the solid wall, the window—like the door or chimney and all the orifices of the house—knows what must enter or leave. Air, wind, and smoke are organized as though they were respirations and living breath. And since nature is so full that it merges with the dwelling, the window only provides a minuscule view.

But from whom or what must one be protected? Others—marauders or sexual predators; natural elements (rain, storms, wind, cold, heat); and animals, whether ferocious or mythic, harmful or sacred. The house and the village turn into citadels because little by little, individuals become aware of the valuables they have, including cattle and cereal harvests, as well as women and the elite. Historians date the first fortification walls to around the fourth millennium. In ancient Rome, Janus, who had a double face, incarnated the one who watches over the entrances and exits of the city. In China, keeping fortifications was the privilege of a particularly devoted vassal. As a strange recompense, his feet were cut off, a radical way to be assured of his fidelity. Some walls protecting a group of seigneurial houses were deified to the point that the heads of freshly slaughtered enemies were buried at their feet as an offering to invigorate them. Thus, from a mythological perspective, the guardians of doors and gates have always had a very important role in both Asia and the West.

In other cultures, honors were given to the builder of walls. In Kabylia, Algeria, in the past, the stonecutter was part of a caste, like the blacksmith. These artisans were the only ones to be honored with the title *ma'allem*, or master. Villagers called on stonecutters to direct the work during construction. But stonecutters also knew how to make grindstones for oil or grain mills, confirming their vital role in the cycles of life. If the house is a sacred place, all who protect it are also sacred, including those who guard and make the fortification walls.

Type of Space

"To go through the door, remain at the door, storm the door." There are many expressions that underline how complicated entering a house can be, especially when one is not really invited.

For aeons, the house has kept the mythic dimension of a consecrated place, in exchange for which the spirits and gods have been given offerings, incantations, and appropriation rites. Thus all of the elements of the building have a meaning. Threshold and door indicate that no one can penetrate just any way into the boundaries defined by the walls: everyone must respect the transfer of this portion of the earth from gods to mortals.

Psychoanalyst Olivier Marc notes that in any architectural space—even the most basic, like that of the Muslims' prayer rug—a notion of access is found. Always turned toward Mecca, this rug has an entrance and an exit. The threshold is very important because it marks the frontier of the premises, separating the profane space from the sacred space, the outer from the inner. But how can this concept be materialized—by walls, fortifications, doors, locks, and keys; by something solid, hard, inaccessible, elevated, or surrounded by water? Is a physical barrier necessary to set the boundaries of one's territory? Anthropologist Edward T. Hall observed that not everyone sees this in the same way. Silence sometimes acts better than a door to set the boundaries of each person's privacy. This is true in Arab houses, where it replaces interior walls. In Japan, these borders were even subtler in the past—not in the interior of the private space, but in the inclusion of the house in the rest of the community, in its relationship with public space. In summer, these blurred boundaries are still at play in Japanese villages. People walk from one place to another, from their house to the general store, dressed in a light blue and white kimono, a *yakuta*, which can almost be described as underclothing. Here it is the network of obligations, social connections, which, now as in the past, takes the place of doors. These are moral barriers that everyone respects if they want to remain in the group. There is nothing to hide in a Japanese house, nothing to steal, either. This particularity can be seen in the country itself, where there are no fortified cities. Thus, the notion of space can also be cultural.

Mauritania, Oualata.
The decorated threshold
of a house: an anteroom
between public and
private space

Opened or Closed

"May your door be opened like a mosque." This Kabyle saying wishes prosperity to its recipient. In this region of Algeria, to enable the sun to fertilize the house, it is better to leave the door opened; when closed, it becomes the symbol of sterility and famine. No one would have the preposterous idea of sitting on the threshold, which could hinder the passage of happiness.

However, in other cultures the threshold is the place for socializing, a required point of passage that marks an intervening space between community life and private life. The opened door reinforces the impression of presence; closed, it testifies to absence. The Chinese knew how to translate such an idea and added to it their own cosmogonic perception of the world. This can be found in their way of transcribing the word *door* using different ideograms. When closed, the door is called *k'ouen*, associated with a passive principle of the earth. When open, it is called *k'ien*, linked to the active principle of the sky. In this way, the door symbolically becomes that which gives rhythm to the universe. Moreover, round "moon doors," found in temple gardens, illustrate quite well the image of a material world always in tune with the natural world—as if a large eye surveys cosmic space.

The Balinese knew how to give doors and gates a certain complexity. Going through one that opens onto a garden, in front of the house, requires a certain protocol and confers to a guest a particular sta-tus. The doors allow guests to show themselves, present themselves, because their low lintel and their narrowness force those entering to take their time, to slow down. Stopping anyone from making an abrupt irruption into a domain that is not theirs, the doors are a tribute to slowness. From the few steps on which the doors are built, the inhabitant can see someone arriving, and—according to a custom inspired by Hinduism—can take care that Brahmans and strangers enter before people of lower castes. But the door that gives access to the house is always opened, whereas, in Bali, protecting the house is necessary. A staggered screen wall plays this role and acts to preserve the privacy of the enclosure.

Among the Wodaabe Tulani, inhabitants of the Sahara desert, the enclosure that protects the house is made of a thorny hedge, which also guards against the sandy winds and provides a little shade. Its entrance always faces west and gives direct access to the corral where the young calves are tied. The animals provide better protection against all intruders than a reinforced door could. They are sensitive to the smallest change and their behavior warns of an intruder's presence. Above all, they form a barrier to be crossed—like the geese that saved Rome's capitol.

Opened or closed, the door guards a mystery, surprising no matter what side you find yourself on. Something known, something unknown—what is behind it?

Mali, Dogon country. The door of the granary and its lock make an arch between humans and the vital grain, *fonio*. Only the blacksmith knows the secret.

Entry Forbidden

There are many ways of defending property, of protecting it from wild animals, insects, or torrential rains. In the mountains of northern Cameroon, the Mofus have turned their concessions—groups of huts where extended families live—into real fortresses. A maze of connected huts provides the inhabitants, their cattle, and their harvests with ingenious protection. The concession is punctuated by doors that you cannot go through without really knowing the place where small walls form partitions.

Many African concessions have only one entrance, which controls arrivals. Sometimes, access to other huts must be made through the chief's hut. Sometimes the huts of the women and children group around this to form a barrier. A similar layout can be found in many villages on the Greek islands, where the houses are inextricably mixed together. On the other hand, in Venezuela, the Piaroas Indians prefer to gather in the community house if there is any danger. Beyond its ritual character, this gathering place serves as the unit for survival and can receive everyone under its roof.

A promontory offers the best protection. In New Guinea, the Korowais built their houses so far from the ground that they go beyond stilts: the access ladder is at least 33 feet (10 meters) high. Above all, building their houses in treetops offers the Korowais protection from the humid and dense jungle. Several families are gathered in two or three perched huts, whose construction demands meticulous care. First, the right tree must be chosen: a banana tree, the solidest of all. After the trunk is pruned, scaffolding is set up to install the floor (made of interwoven branches covered with palm bark). The walls are erected using stalks of the sago palm, and the roof is made using its leaves. Finally, the scaffolding is taken down, and there only remains a long pole to serve as a staircase. Different peoples who have built their houses on stilts explain that in equatorial climates this enables better ventilation and protects from flooding. When built on water, the houses enable inhabitants to have fish at their fingertips. No matter how these bearing stilts are used and how the house is accessed—by boat, stairs, or bridge—height is essential.

Indonesia, Irian Jaya.
The houses are built 98, sometimes 164, feet (30/50 meters) from the ground, to escape wild animals and the rains that regularly transform the forest into a swamp.

Yemen, Bayt Bawz.
The house, like an
impregnable citadel

Strange Guardians

Long ago in China, it was thought that evil spirits wandered through houses. The only recourse was to invite guardians that were just as powerful. To accomplish this, glazed ceramics or figurines with animal forms were placed at each end of the roof. In imperial cities, huge dragons, measuring 10 feet (3 meters) high and weighing about 3 tons, stood watch among other guardians. These statues, designed to suit the stature of their illustrious inhabitant, were called *tunjishou*, "beasts that devour fate." Naturally, the more important and powerful the person to be protected, the greater the number and size of the beasts. Always found in odd numbers, these figurines sometimes looked like a real procession: fish, lion, phoenix, horse, etc. The geomancers also advised those who inhabited evil premises, like coffin merchants or coal stockers, to place mirrors above doors and roofs, or in bedrooms, to detect evil influences and chase them away.

In the Berbers' world in Morocco, one can often find the hand of Fātimah. It has protective virtues and is hung on houses with horseshoes, thorns, or stones. First, however, a lamb is sacrificed for protection from dangerous jinn. Stuffed lizards or plaits of wheat are also valuable talismans, gauges of prosperity for the family and of fertility for the women. It is considered a good omen to have a turtle in your home or to let a snake wander there. (In central India, women mold imprints of calves on

China, Guizhou-Guangxi Province. Colorful ceramic monkeys decorate the roofs.

the threshold or in the footprints of guests to attract luck.)

People who live under an animist conception of the world—where plants, animals, and objects act as a bridge between gods and mortals—are always careful to put their dwellings under the best omens. In Morocco, an old olive or nut tree plays the role of protector. In Mongolia, a few hairs from a horse's mane, or a silk scarf attached to a post that is carved and decorated with drawings, are used. When nomads take down the *gher*, they take care to place the posts in the direction of their future campsite, because an ancestral belief attributes a sacred and protective character to this wood, which acts on the tent. In the Japanese countryside, a cauldron suspended over the hearth—from a post decorated with the ideogram for water, *mizu*—prevents fires. It is often believed that naming a thing or representing it will confer a power on it. For this reason, Chinese carpenters put fireproof charms on the roof frames. The ceramic owl that acts to keep away storms at the time of the solstice, and which is actually a lightning rod, was perhaps more efficient. On the ridgepoles of pavilions and pagodas, one can find an egg-shaped object called a "mandarin bud," similar to the "civil servant's hat." It protects from storms and lightning. Thus, at all times and in every context, in the face of inexplicable phenomena, humans have had recourse to different fetishes or rites to implore the evil spirits to spare their houses.

China, Guizhou-Guangxi Province. Divinities were installed on the roofs of dwellings to protect their inhabitants from evil influences or natural disasters such as lightning and fire.

Divine Protection

In Jewish houses, a mezuzah is sometimes hung from the door lintel. It contains a small, sacred parchment roll referring to an episode in the Torah, which gives it a divine presence. Everyone touches the mezuzah when entering or leaving the house. In this way, it has become a kind of guardian of the household. In India, this role is taken up by a colored mandala, a type of "ritual labyrinth" painted by the women, in the courtyard of the house. For Hindus, the mandala, signifying the circle, is a representation of the divine at the center of the world. It is divided into four and nine boxes dedicated to the divinities Shiva and Parvati, the mythological "holy family." The middle is reserved for the chamber womb of Brahma, the creator god. Other rows of squares have a connection with the cycles of the moon and sun. This same diagram is found in the organization of temples. The mandala makes the house sacred.

In the Andes, to avoid offending the divinities that protect the house, a ritual celebration is consecrated to them in August, the month of *Pachamama*, Mother Earth. A hole is dug in the middle of the courtyard, where drinks and food are placed. A white stone marks the spot, and every year Pachamama is nourished again so that it rains and the earth is fertile, and the herds are in good health.

In the Bulgan region of Mongolia, a lamb is sacrificed to bless the house. As a souvenir of this ritual, a piece of meat offered to the divinity of the hearth is hung on a post.

The Chinese pantheon has gods specialized in the protections of exits. Qin-Shubao and Hu Jingde resemble two ferocious generals armed with axes and halberds. Beginning in the seventh century, their effigy—carved into peach-tree wood, a symbol of immortality—was placed on the doors to frighten evil spirits. Images of the cock were also used to protect against epidemics, misfortunes, and disasters. In Chinese the word for cock, *ji*, is a homophone for "good omen" or "lucky."

In the past, all these ritual and religious acts were not without an echo in the Christian West. The blessing of houses, and of crosses decorated with boxwood, by evoking Christ's victory over death, acquired a value as protectors from evil. On the outside walls, the statues of saints placed in a niche were also a way of imploring for protection from the beyond.

India. Woman drawing a mandala—a meditation aid and religious representation of the world

Need for Privacy

How do we define privacy, and at what point is it considered threatened? Every culture has a different idea of respectful visual and aural distances, and of restricted space—whether or not walls delimit it. The notion of privacy is sometimes linked to more delicate parameters. In Japan, where the walls of a traditional house are made from light wood and paper—earthquakes throughout the centuries have given rise to stronger materials—the inhabitants have a great tolerance for what we would call nuisances. Noise is part of the environment, since space is shared. A partition is pulled and a bedroom is created; a couch is pushed back and it becomes a bed. Space is fluid, and privacy must follow. It's up to each person to know how to be alone despite a saturated visual and aural world. This aptitude allows the Japanese to handle life in a group without perceiving it, for the most part, as a restriction of their personal freedom. Thus, they have the habit of not talking too loud so as not to bother their neighbors. On the other hand, according to anthropological observations regarding space, Germans are intolerant of noise, so they adopted double walls and padded doors a long time ago. Another way of turning down the volume!

Private space also brings into play a way of looking at others without disturbing them. There is a specific distance to respect, depending on where you find yourself on the planet. Moving furniture or touching objects, when you are not at home, is sometimes a sacrilegious act, to the point that furniture that cannot be lifted has been designed to separate different interior spaces. However, these cultural codes are not always easy to decipher. Any traveler needs to know how to respect the privacy of others, in order to be invited to share it.

Cameroon, the Koma people. The opening of the hut is the passageway between two worlds, the known and the unknown, the shadow and the light.

Access Codes

In the Muslim world, there is often a distinction made between public and private behavior. Outside the house, under the eyes of others, a person does not really belong to him or herself. In any case, the street, the souk, is a place where the body is seen, whereby exposing oneself to the group, the individual runs the risk of putting him or herself in danger, of being coveted or envied. Some cultures have preferred to build symbolic walls around women, who here wear a *hidjab* outside, a covering whose name means "protection." For the more affluent, domestic architecture is an attempt to enlarge private space; patios, high ceilings, and spacious and cleared rooms let the inhabitants gather together while keeping their integrity—away from outside looks.

Builders had to resolve many other problems to reconcile two values: hospitality and honor (*horma*), a word that in Arabic means "privacy," "dignity," and "integrity," all at the same time. This ensemble governs the basic laws of the house, which, transformed into a real shell, is thought—above all—to protect the inhabitants.

The vestibule then becomes a room of primary importance. The Arab-Andalusian houses of Morocco have a type of judas hole. If there is any doubt about the sex of a guest—division between men's and women's space being strict at times—it is up to the guest to announce him or herself by crying out, coughing, or whistling. In Yemen, when a male who is a stranger to the family descends the staircase, women are warned by a crying out of the name of God, so that they can slip away. When a Yemenite man enters the house, the women are obliged to leave the common space; he stoops to pass through a door that is too low for him in a symbolic gesture of his allegiance to the rules of the place. More and more often, two staircases are found—one for each sex—to be sure the two won't encounter each other. In addition, from a second-floor promontory overlooking the street, Yemenite women of Sanaa can open and close the entrance door to the house as they please using a cord connected to the locks. A kind of surveillance camera combined with an intercom—ahead of its time!

Above: India. Window with openwork panels—a way of seeing without being seen

Opposite: Yemen, Buqur. Windows with different forms and functions

Spiritual Barrier

"We warn you, Father Spirit and Mother Spirit, that a friend is visiting." With this phrase, accompanied by the offerings of candles and flowers, some Laotians demand permission from the spirits of their parents to receive guests in the house. A curious custom related by ethnologists Sophie and Pierre Clément, which makes sense when you are aware that the ancestors, even after their death, are always considered the owners of their lodging. The inheritors are only tenants, and the rules that direct the house are a way of respecting this tacit pact between the living and the dead. The architecture has been adapted to this concept. Thus, some rooms are strictly off-limits to strangers—like the bedroom, the place of privacy par excellence. The room containing the family altar is protected by a type of screen. The staircase is a natural obstacle: by changing floors, you penetrate into a new space. Before committing a blunder, you have time to become aware of it—or to stop the momentum of the impolite guest. The private areas of a house are thus spared.

Ethnologists noted in their study on the Vientiane houses in Loas that to this opposition of spaces can be added the opposition of light. The bedroom made of braided bamboo is not very exposed to light, while the living room and kitchen are always bright. Light and dark respond to the duality of opened and closed.

Two types of windows are also found: through one you can see while standing up, through the other, only when seated. Choosing when you see or are seen is another way of preserving privacy. In many Mediterranean houses, terraced roofs enable the somewhat contradictory situation of "being inside and outside at the same time." The inhabitant can observe the street as he or she wishes without the risk of being seen, which seems essential in cultures where the mixing of the sexes is not easy. The balcony, immortalized by Shakespeare in *Romeo and Juliet*, fulfills this function: one sees and is seen without overstepping the barriers of privacy. Honor is saved!

Opposite: China, Guizhou-Guangxi Province. In cultures where the mixing of the sexes is regulated, the balcony lets inhabitants avoid unexpected meetings.

Following pages: India, Jodhpur. The terraced roofs allow a person to be outside while remaining in a private sphere.

History of Windows

In Ghana, windows are sometimes reduced to a minuscule opening that lets air circulate while keeping the room cool. In cold countries, the inhabitants try to let as little air in as possible.

However, the history of windows is also connected to the history of their environment. The openings are enlarged when possessions and inhabitants seem safe.

It must be recalled that in many cultures, aeration is avoided out of fear of letting occult forces enter or escape. These peoples like to be away from drafts, in the half-light. Some obscure currents of Western medicine in the nineteenth century recommended breathing the tainted air of drafts to avoid infections. Throughout the centuries, before the stained-glass window, embedded in plaster, was adopted from the Arabs, numerous attempts were made to fit windows. Every conceivable material was tested: oiled paper, linen, white stone, horn, parchment, pork bladder. Finally in the seventh century, Germans combined know-how and technology to make the prototypes of our present-day windows. Glass was then so rare and expensive that the nobility transported it from one castle to another. To protect the openings better, they used heavy curtains. In the West, until the appearance of the bow window, looking at the landscape was a real luxury. In Yemen, an entire room in the house was devoted to the window. Men received their friends there and chewed khat, a local herb with psychotropic properties. To make stained glass, the Yemenite masons used gypsum rock, a very strong material. Heated to a high temperature, it provided a white coating used to decorate the facades. But the masons could also spread this paste and, after letting it dry, cut it with a knife in the shape of the windowpanes. All that was left to do was to insert the colored glass. As a superb refinement, some had a screen wall of plaster made in front of their window, slightly shifted back from the windowpane: this diffused a filtered light during the hours of full sun.

Opposite: India, Himachal Pradesh. Spiti Valley. Letting in air and light

Following pages: Nepal, Bhaktapur. Palace with elaborate carved windows

Air and Water

If the large huts of the Wodaabes of Nigeria do not need any special opening, it is because the straw they are made from is open enough to air and light to let what is necessary filter through. Coolness is most important, because for these inhabitants of the desert, it is essential to be protected from sun (and sandstorms). The entrance door is on the side opposite the dominant winds. Made of grass and sewn plaits, this unique door modifies the direction of air streams, acting as a channeler.

Windows, on the other hand, are found in all shapes in the city of Sanaa, Yemen. Decorated with brick or plaster, they all have a different function. The *lustres*, with their small squares in a row, light only the stairs; they testify to the mason's special talent for capturing light. The *oculina*, from the Latin *eye*, are small round windows set in alabaster that spread a soft light through their colored panes. The bay window, framed with carved wooden shutters, is installed at floor level in the main living room—a room that is always located on the second floor of the house. *Shâqûs* are tiny orifices that let air circulate through the house. Other skylights transform into hood pipes and act as kitchen chimneys.

While the window provides light and air everywhere in Senegal, for the Diolas of lower Casamance, it also serves to collect rainwater. Over a large earthen tub, it looks like a hole in the middle of the house and echoes a Roman *impluvium*. Its central position in the roof lets it diffuse light throughout. There is daylight in the atrium and veranda that surrounds it, half-light in the kitchen and bedrooms, and complete darkness in the granaries—which keeps the grain from germinating. It is sometimes a challenge to organize space based on light—certainly when there is no electricity, as is often the case.

Senegal, *impluvium* hut. This particular window lets in light and collects rainwater.

Honorable Distinctions

Giving a house a name shows its uniqueness. "Enough for Me," "My Dream," "Little Treasure," these pleasant names, in forged iron, are sometimes written on the gable walls of vacation houses, especially in France. In China, where the language has more imagery and is perhaps more apt at metaphor, the portals bear indications such as "Great Gate," "Garden of Trees and Flowers," "Great Official," according to the prestige of the inhabitants. The former Han family included everyone who was part of an economic unit, all generations together, with several couples and their children. Rich families extended further to include those who served or worked there: servants, farm laborers, disciples of the educated, artisans' apprentices, and merchants' assistants. The Chinese word *hou* (household) designates all of these people and even includes dead grandparents. The typical Chinese expression "to be under the flagpole" means that one of these members was particularly distinguished, by being

Mali, Dogon country. Animal skins are hung on a sorcerer's house.

successful at exams, by being a prosperous tradesman, or by having earned the title of mandarin. A streamer is hung in front of the door to commemorate all these illustrious titles, or they are engraved in letters of gold or cinnabar—red sulfite of mercury—on black wooden boards. The neighborhood then respects every member of this household— even the pets. In return, the family must show itself worthy of these distinctions and try to surpass them.

In Tibet, anyone who owns a collection of sacred Buddhist books places a wooden cone and a special piece of fabric on their roof as an exterior sign of wisdom.

For certain ethnic groups of Cameroon, only important personages have the right to put carved doors on their entrances. The greater their respectability, the more decorated doors they have. However, unless they are a part of the royal family, the nobility cannot build more than two doors. You have to earn these decorations.

Guinea-Bissau, Bijagós Archipelago, Canhabaque. A monkey indicates the direction of the entrance.

The Useful and Pleasant

Not so long ago in Ghana, to pay homage to their dead spouses, princes' wives painted the black-and-white patterns that had decorated their husbands' loincloths on the concessions of their hamlets. After coating the walls with white chalk, a symbol of purity, they added tar mixed with sand and water. Once the water evaporated, this mixture served as an antiseptic by making the earthen wall impermeable.

In villages in West Africa, the decoration of exterior walls is often the work of women, who give free rein to their imaginations. Some mothers do not hesitate to represent the perils that lie in wait for their children. Like a colorful warning, they draw scorpions or snakes whose bites are deadly. In Japan, such incitements to prudence are sometimes inscribed in houses' interiors. Carved on wood, one of the most renowned is a dog warning its pup of the danger of fire. Animals are always honored in Japan, where it is thought that an agreeable *kawai*, or image associated with an idea, is remembered more easily. The famous cat, *maneki neko*, literally "making a sign to enter," has been the shop sign of merchants for years. Placed in the window like a lucky charm, it acts as a mascot.

In the Indian Himalaya, villagers apply pats of yak dung to houses' facades. Though this decoration seems surprising, it is very practical. The dried dung is used as fuel in this region, where wood is scarce. A few mountains away, their Tibetan neighbors decorate their roofs with prayer flags that form a long banner, as a reminder that meditation is higher than the mundane activities of mortals. In Ghana, aesthetically pleasing grooves are carved into the walls of huts to help drain rainwater. A few stalks of millet are always left above the entrance door to dry before being offered on a dish to guests.

India, Thar Desert.
Floral designs painted
with rice paste

All Kinds of Patterns

Zigzags for the legs of gazelles, triangles for the wings of bats, parallel lines for furrows, circles for cola nuts: these are a few examples of the decorative designs of West African huts. In the chieftainships of Cameroon, decorated posts mark the status and greatness of their owners as much as they support the buildings' awnings. Representations of the king and queen and their servants attest that one is before the house of a dignitary. Animals are commonly represented on African doors and facades of concessions. In an animistic vision, the animal is invested with a quasi-totemic value and evokes, if not the founding mythologies, the emblem of a family or an entire clan. These patterns have a social and religious significance.

For the Bamilekes of Cameroon, the snake, associated with the image of woman, is a sign of fertility. Because of its form—symbolically linked to the phallus—and the deadly power of its venom, it is said to oscillate between life and death. The croco-dile is also a much-esteemed totem. It usually incarnates fertile power, while the ox, panther, and elephant represent bravery and virility. The chameleon indicates trickery; the spider, knowledge; and the turtle—whose stylized checkered shell is a pattern used frequently in Cameroon by the Betis and in Fang art—intelligence.

As to pure forms, their references must be looked for in cosmologies. The circle shows the world as a whole, symbolizes the sun, or, when topped with a cross, represents the cardinal points. The earth is circular and so is water: all things circular are divine. For the Ibo of Nigeria, the circle references a legend in which emissaries were sent to earth four days a week by the gods, on a four-day walk that gives rhythm to the week. Along the frieze on the facades, the triangle and diamond (apparently feminine shapes), like the square and rectangle, alternate with the image of the cosmos, the stars, and the moon.

Left: Niger. Leather tent decorated with colorful geometric designs

Opposite: Niger. Decorations sculpted on the wall of a house

Coded Message

For the Bonis in Guyana, the drawings on the main wall and the entrance doors cannot be read easily. The association of different patterns forms messages with a connotation that is often sexual. The rose windows represent women's navels and the interlacing of lines denotes an embrace. These decorative metaphors testify to a patient know-how. The content is often not very serious: a message of love or an explicit invitation to join the man inside—whose house represents his status as adult.

The objects represented on the walls also have their own symbolic value. They often indicate prosperity; in Ghana they simply indicate the hut's owner or usage. Thus, gourds are painted on women's huts, and pipes, canes, or the braids worn by old people are represented on the huts of ancestors. Materials are often woven on the same model and the patterns for body drawings also recall these geometric variations.

Niger. The designs are not purely decorative; they often have a symbolic function.

China, Karakol Lake. Kirghiz tents. Their whiteness is a sign of wealth.

The Color of Prestige

Formerly, in Mongolia, young women prepared the decorations for their future *gher*, up until the day of their marriage. The fabrication of felt was also the prerogative of women. All of central Asia used felt, according to historians, who found evidence of its use in Altai, Siberia, thirteen thousand years ago. Turkish shepherds from southern Anatolia had a veritable housecoat, the *képének* (a large, heavy felt cape). Using their staff, they transformed it into a small tent, where they could spend the night when going to summer pastures. The Mongols, like all Asian nomads, used felt to cover the roof of their gher. Today this fabric, made of sheep's wool and sometimes camel's hair, is bought in sheets. Previously, animal breeders made this agglomeration of wool themselves. Its color is still its most important feature. For the Mongols, *tsagaan*, meaning both "white" and "happy," inhabits all favorable things. The felt of the gher must keep this immaculate color, which brings happiness, as long as possible. To keep its purity in spite of rain and dust, the gher has to be renovated every five years. But not all nomads have the necessary means. Therefore, the color of the gher shows social status. A well-maintained house that the neighbors can see is proof of opulence everywhere.

For Mediterranean civilizations, purple, a very rare color, was often given a place of honor, reserved for the clothing of the nobility, and for drapes and rugs that decorated the house. It is true that this color was the most complicated to make, because the dye had to be extracted from marine gastropods Murex and Purpura. At least twelve thousand of these creatures have to be fished to obtain one gram of coloring. In Buddhist tradition, violet goes beyond the opposites and the complementary natures of yin and yang. It is the most sacred color. Therefore it is never found on the facades of houses, but it decorates sacred places, flags, and the pediments of temples.

Rainbow

Red, associated with the color of blood, and therefore, with life, has always been preferred by certain peoples of the world. Some sewed a red thread in their clothing for protection; others painted red house openings. In China, a red door could have a beneficial effect on the entire dwelling.

In Mongolia, traveling painters offered to decorate the doors of *ghers*. They chose different colored patterns, with a preference for blue, the symbol of longevity. The Berbers of Morocco tried to defend windows against occult intrusions. Using a mixture of ocher, yellow or red, the women decorated windows with the same patterns used in henna tattoos—which protected certain body parts. In China, people liked most of all to decorate the colored and varnished tile roofs, creating a coded rainbow. According to Michel Culas, an object specialist in China, local architects have always given importance to roofs. "Flying roofs," with their shape of thrusting corners, can appear yellowish gold, red, navy blue, watery green, turquoise, or eggplant purple. However, these special decorations were reserved for mansions belonging to the nobility. Yellow was often the color of imperial buildings: it was considered the color of the earth and, therefore, of the center and, in consequence, of the emperor. Green was reserved for the royal family, and black was used for libraries; since this color corresponded to the element water, it would protect them better from fires. In this way, each color had its meaning—though beauty often needed no other justification than the pleasure it gave.

Left: China. Red, a beneficial color, brings happiness and prosperity.

Opposite: China. Color codes define the social group to which the household belongs.

Noble Forms

Like the choice of color or pattern, the choice of material is an exterior sign of wealth. Mosaics, alcoves, cut stone, sculpted plaster, and finely wrought wood are so many architectural details that can speak about the opulence of inhabitants. Columns visibly inspire builders of large mansions, whether Indian or Florentine. Whether painted or formed, arches that the visitor must contemplate or pass through to arrive at the master's house carry a rich symbolism. Columns represent the axis of the construction, the solidity, even a triumphant self-affirmation close to the phallic erection. The ancient Greeks gave a more poetic definition: the column is, above all, the schematization of a tree. The column's base marks the roots, its shaft, the trunk, and its capital, the leaves, making it a direct reference to the tree of life. For those who would be tempted to decorate their balconies with gold plating, the *Dictionary of Symbols* states that gold is for Buddhists the color of absolute perfection, for Chinese, the color of knowledge, and for Indians, the color of immortality. For the Bambara and Dogon in Mali, it is the "materialization of the original vibration" and for Louis XIV and the princes of all civilizations, it is the color of divinity and royalty.

But in Morocco and Andalusia, the studded entrance doors, floor tiling, plaster cornices, wrought-iron balconies, and painted wood are only visible to those who enter. A very wise attitude; and one that some Indians have understood, because they prefer their resting cushion, the *gaddi*, to be only slightly higher than that of the poor. This is certainly the surest way of avoiding covetousness.

Iraq. Teahouse reserved for men, completely built of woven reeds

West Africa. Decorating the dwelling is often an activity for women.

Fabrication Secret

African women transmit from generation to generation the know-how for using their hands like a brush to decorate houses. These family secrets are whispered from mother to daughter: "Find clay from the rivers that will resist rain and sun; find inspiration in sayings to draw on the walls; repair cracks with a mixture of excrements; draw a good python to protect a newborn." And if the hand is their first tool, what of the stones, feathers, millet and sorghum, shards of bottles, and pieces of gourds that make them outstanding artisans? In India, in the state of Orissa, the women find a use for the least particle of their rice harvest. With the stalks, they cover the roofs, and with the bad grains, they make a white paste to cover the dark earthen walls—which they decorate with arabesques of climbing plants and flower buds. To bless their dwelling, they place a saffron pistil on the doorstep

West Africa. Pieces of broken dishes taken from the environment are used to personalize the home.

in homage to Lakshmi, the goddess of prosperity.

In Oualata, Mauritania, people strive to multiply geometric shapes out of respect for the Koranic instructions that prohibit any human representation. The women have become experts in the art of handling the knife that they use to carve door and window frames. The wealthier the family, the more decorated the wall. Mural painting is also a collective tradition for West African women. A woman who wants to decorate her house enlists the help of others, who coat the facades with a mixture of earth and cow dung, then scrape down the surface with a urine mixture. Next, the owner paints the first pattern and the others follow with their own inspirations.

In France, the makers of the Roman tiles that cover the roofs of many homes have their own little secrets. Their very particular semicircular shape was achieved by modeling the clay over their thighs.

The Course of Life

The houses where we are born and spend our childhood often have the charm of nostalgia. They compel us to journey back or to return for good. Some have a soul where the happiness and the pain of living confront each other. Even abandoned, they are never really empty. They carry traces and imprints testifying to their past life. But the dilapidation of a space always seems strange, troubling, and confusing, because it is felt as a foreshadowing of death or the return to chaos. To protect themselves from death, the living often reserve a place for the dead, near the hearth. Where will the spirit of the departed go if not to its own home? Where could it be better off?

For the Romans, the protective divinities, or Penates, guard the threshold of the house. The sprites of Scandinavia, France, and elsewhere are also part of the household. In Britain, they are reserved the best place, near the hearth,

Mongolia. A mix of all generations at a family meal inside a *gher*

around which people gather together in the evening to soothe them. In this way, save for occasional tricks, they are thought to sweep the kitchen at night, grind grain, or churn butter, and were compensated with a cup of milk. Even though the spirits of the house play tricks, enjoy moving objects, and make the beams and floorboards creak, once their benevolence is gained through offerings, perfect cohabitation can ensue. The spirits of the hearth are the most honored because fire is vital for cooking and heating. It repels wild animals and insects. Its presence reassures and keeps the wandering evil powers at a distance. On New Year's Day, the great housecleaning chases them out, but they should not stop longevity, prosperity, and happiness from entering. In this way, the house has a new skin for rebirth. Something new, unexpected, and possible starts during the ritual celebration of the New Year, beneficial for the dwelling and the people in it.

Similarly, the birth of a child gives rise to protection rites. Superstitions and mythologies are mixed with the fear of death during childbirth and infant mortality. Throughout the world, eight out of ten children are born outside of a hospital. At home or out in the open—the mother gives birth where she feels the safest and most confident. What other choice does she have when access to medical help is impossible? People employ any means to keep away the evil spirits that could harm the life of the newborn—the most precious thing. Fire, milk, and salt are among the protective barriers used. In France, recourse to the protection of Our Lady of Deliverance, Relief, and the Seven Sorrows is an echo of these practices. Women in labor carry talismans, amulets, and medals, while the images of saints are frequently hung on the drapes of the bedroom where the birth takes place.

Though the worlds of spirits, humans, and animals naturally come together in a dwelling, each one stays in its place. Animals sometimes represent the only wealth of a family, and their fate is linked to that of the humans. Thus, they are kept close by, where they can be seen and heard.

Private Space

How can space be shared, divided according to the activities and necessities of each person? In designing a house, every architect asks some basic questions. The traditional habitat offered precise answers to the needs of those it sheltered, always referring to their vision of the world. But all cultures are not in agreement on the sacred aspects of the actions involved in living. In India, practicing Hindus can only be born, make love, or die on the ground, in direct contact with Mother Earth—not in a bed. In Japan, perhaps to feel the elements more, people live, eat, and sleep by preference on tatamis, small braided rugs made of rice straw. A room is reserved for this purpose, built accord-ing to traditional standards. In its design, the tatami resembles a kimono, which is also made of bands of equal length that are added or taken away according to life's events. This particular evolution is connected again to the idea that the house and the body are superimposed. Consequently, it seems normal that in the tatami room, precise rules are obeyed to satisfy the requirements of a life on the ground. Removing shoes to enter the house is more than a custom: it is an act coherent with Buddhist thought. It allows the home to be preserved from the dirt of the outside world. Not putting one's feet on a table, nor shoes on a bed, fulfills the same purpose.

Yemen. Family meal. The division of rooms corresponds with social organization.

In Kabyle villages in Algeria, it was formerly the custom to divide houses' space into two sections. One was dark, low, and humid; the other, bright, elevated, and dry. Some years ago, sociologist Pierre Bourdieu studied this phenomenon thoroughly. He relates that a person sleeps, conceives, gives birth, and dies in the first space and eats, works, and receives guests in the second. He observes that these spaces act as communicating vessels. During the day, the living room is full and busy; when night falls, all the living beings of the house gather around the stable: cows, sheep, oxen, and humans mixed together. It shelters all kinds of activities, even the most private. For good reason, this place remains the most intimate part of the house. It is a secret and fecund place. The place where one dies is the place where one is born, since every birth is a rebirth of a deceased person and a part of the eternal return.

Following the same logic of division of space, the mountain people of Kabyle have developed the habit of storing objects according to their attributes. Jars filled with water and grains reserved for sowing are stored in a dark section, sometimes under the conjugal bed, while cereals reserved for cooking are stored high up in a dry spot near the hearth.

Amazonia, Serra de Surucucu. For the Yanomami, the hammock defines everyone's personal space.

The House Where One Is Born

For the Inuit of the Arctic, since the house is associated with the womb, it is natural that women give birth there. The men are careful to level the threshold in front of the igloo door, to ease pain and symbolically facilitate the passage of the child. In Laos, according to the same logic, all hanging objects are taken down in order to get rid of things that could obstruct the baby's arrival. In Morocco, when the woman's water breaks, there is a custom of pouring water over the threshold of the door so that it runs toward the interior to insure that "everything goes well." It is an act of purification or offering to the spirits of the house, a sign of welcome intended to make the life forces favorable. In Mongolia, to give birth, women hang on to the *bagana*, one of the posts of the *gher* that circles the hearth. Made of birch, a sacred tree the shamans use for ceremonies, this pole links the earth to the sky like a cosmic axis, and it is thought that its beneficial forces pass from mother to child. The Japanese slide a paper dog under their pillow to facilitate delivery and devour any sicknesses that could lie in wait for the child. In Africa, the baby must be born in its grandmother's house to benefit from good auspices: the shades of ancestors live there and have the power to protect the newborn. For the Basuto of Lesotho, grandparents also play an important role. They are the ones who take care of the child during its first years. The Dogon of Mali build a house reserved for giving birth, in the heart of the village, a way of inducting the child into the group from the time it is born. Everyone participates in the event, and the community accepts the child right away as one of its members, by publicly reciting its genealogy. For the Navajo, birth is also a community event. At each birth, the entire village comes together around a large banquet to help. This custom is also practiced in the Basque Provinces of Spain where an opened place is preferred over the protection of a house. A riverbank is often chosen for giving life—water being a symbol of fertility—and people dance and sing, enjoying themselves until the baby arrives. In Yemen, even though a woman gives birth at home, she is visited by many neighbors and friends who comfort her during labor. This is similar to the customs of the Maya Indians in the Yucatán. On her hammock, the mother-to-be converses with her family, isolated by a simple fabric. Practical solutions and efficient methods must be found when there are no doctors around.

Yemen. A room of the
house is usually reserved
for giving birth.

A Separate Room

In the Amazon rainforest, the *kaluwat* are legendary creatures that hide in the rocky peaks and lure us to the "earth without evil," or sweet paradise, if we do not know how to resist them. Only the shaman can control them, and their arrival is dreaded at each momentous event, where they could break the precarious balance between gods and mortals. This is why the Emerillon Indians have designed a house reserved for giving birth. The women remain there with the newborn until the baby is more robust—the time it takes for the kaluwat to give up the idea of seizing the baby's soul.

Because birth goes back to the enigma of origins, in many traditional cultures pregnancy removes the mother and child from social life. This keeps the group from being "tainted" by blood, often thought of as impure. Special dwellings, food taboos, and purification rites protect from natural and supernatural dangers. In medieval Europe, noble women retired the month before giving birth to a room whose decorations, drapes, cushions, and covers they made. On an altar, a priest—one of the few people, along with the husband, allowed to visit—came to say mass. Arapesh women in New Guinea and Japanese women live separately in wood cabins at this time. In Laos, some Thai women stay at home, but leave the room where they give birth to be near to the hearth. They purify themselves near the fire, their child resting on a special mattress at their side for a week up to a month, depending on whether the newborn is the first child.

In northern Togo, for the Tambermas, the arrival of a child is considered to be the rebirth of a dead relative. Its room, thought to be as protective as the placenta, is given the greatest care. For seven mornings, with the help of the family's oldest woman, the birth is replayed by passing the baby headfirst through a round window. The baby then lives for six months in a room set up on the terrace; the first, or ground, floor is a sacred place, reserved for ancestors—and it must be respected. Such are the rules that the child learns as it grows.

Togo, Koulankou.
After the birth of a child, the Tambermas make the baby relive the experience: for seven days, the child's head is put out of a round window built for this purpose.

Changing Floors

Rooms are sometimes dedicated to a particular age, sex, or activity, and builders sometimes leave some indication to mark that. In traditional Berber dwellings in Morocco, the man-woman identity is inscribed in the girder and the main post; the first is associated with the head of the family, the second with his spouse. At the time of the girder's installation—often on the couple's wedding day—the part of the foreskin cut during circumcision is hung on it. This beam ends on a forked branch of a tree, which in some regions is given the feminine name Masauda, "the happy one." Beam and post thus symbolize the coupling. In Kabylia, Algeria, as sociologist Pierre Bourdieu noted, sterile women wound their belts around this beam, a symbol of virility that was endowed with magic properties. To hear it crack was a bad omen, announcing the death of a family member. As for young boys, at births the others wished for them "to be the girder of the house," and when they were old enough to participate in the Ramadan fast, they took their meals on the terrace roof, just above this famous beam, so that they could become men.

In Arab-Andalusian houses, the terrace was mostly reserved for women, and was a place for communication from which men were excluded. But the men had at their disposal a reception room on the ground floor. Here the women were associated with the sky and the men with the earth; the opposite was true in Kabyle houses.

In Nepal, the different floors are not distinguished by sex as much as they are by activity. Traditional houses have three floors, where the stairway represents a main axis. Men and women try to find their place between the first floor, reserved for animals; the second floor, for family life; and the terrace, where grain and cereal stalks are threshed.

India, Varanasi. Terraces are often the domain of the women and children, far from the sight of men outside the family.

Making a Place

In German, the word for fruit, *Obst*, has the same etymology as words linked to obstetrics. Traditionally, at each birth a tree was planted in the garden of the family house. This custom inscribed the newborn in a lineage, bestowed on the child a territory, and "rooted" him or her in a culture. The symbolic act of being rooted to the native earth is found throughout the world. In Nigeria, on the outskirts of some villages, each tree of a banana plantation carries the name of a child, and the place serves as a playground. Besides this natural inscription, the house is often the first thing to whom the baby is presented.

In Kabylia, Algeria, one of the eldest women of the community presides at the ceremonies. The *qibla* is in charge of welcoming the newborn. She shows it to the spirits of the house, six times and in six different places where the family has already carried out the rites of blessing the dwelling. Next, she buries the placenta, under a fig tree if the baby is a boy, and under a pomegranate if it is a girl. The fruits of these trees stand for fertility.

For the Tepehuas Indians of Mexico, whatever the child's sex, the dirt floor is turned over and the placenta buried inside the house with salt and tobacco, two vital elements. Elsewhere, in Africa, the placenta is cooked, cut into small pieces and incorporated into the food to give vigor back to the woman after childbirth. In Bali, the placenta finds its place next to the entrance door of the house, buried in a carved coconut. The threshold is one of the magic places of the Balinese house; it is perceived as the place where good and evil forces oppose one another. In the mountains of Morocco, placentas are buried at each birth under the entrance doorstep. By leaving a double of the child to the jinn, the Berbers hope to distract the evil spirits. The Minangkabaus of Sumatra do the same thing for a completely different reason: to stop the child from wandering off. Implanted in this way, they will always know how to find their way back home. For some African ethnicities, it is useless to attach oneself to the house of one's birth—a house of windows and roof—because finally, we have only one dwelling place, to which our soul will return, and that is the placenta. How else could we return to our origins?

Egypt, Cairo. Special protection rites take place in the house where a new child was born.

Bodyguard

Before a birth, some women bustle about the house to fill in all the cracks through which cunning spirits could infiltrate. Superstition or mythology, it is true that the newborn is biologically, socially, and magically incapable of defending itself. All that can be done to reassure a child, who is abruptly hurled into a world not yet his or hers, is quite important. Zulu women in South Africa decorate the place where they give birth with pearls and carved wood, so the child, by being born in magical contact with beauty, will discover the harmony of the universe without violence. Houses in the Maghreb are purified to fight against the evil eye. In Morocco, a cock's head is hung on the entrance door. This animal, a symbol of vigilance in Nordic countries, is also the preferred animal of the prophet in Muslim countries, where it is called "the enemy of the enemy of God." Its crowing informs everyone of an angel's presence. What could be better to protect an infant?

In Thailand, traditional village women about to give birth fill their rooms with special amulets, fabrics, and magic images. The legitimate fears of dying in childbirth and of losing the child have always given rise to magical or religious practices.

In the Atlas Mountains of North Africa, when a mother must leave her child alone, she pours a few drops of milk around the bed and in the four corners of the room as a protective barrier. She nourishes the jinn through this act, turning them away from their prey. A piece of fabric, bearing a little earth from the house—or other amulets—is also hung around the child's neck. The best-known amulets are amber, pieces of metal, verses of the Koran, and blood of a lamb killed at the Aïd feast. They act by transferring sacred power, and are practiced by all cultures, since the life of a child is a very precious possession. Salt, purifier and preserver of foods, plays a role in these rituals. In the Maghreb, it is spread everywhere to assure happiness and bliss, and as a sign of hospitality and shared friendship. In Japan, Shintoist rites recommend it; a divinity, dirtied by a stay in hell, washed itself upon its return by diving into the sea. Consequently, some people throw a little salt on the threshold everyday, while others use it after a funeral or to chase away negative waves of an undesirable person who has stayed in the house. Protecting your home like this is, at the same time, a way of blessing all its occupants.

Russia, Siberia, Yamal region. Under a tent, a Nenet baby is suspended in its cradle surrounded by talismans.

Under the Same Roof

Husbands, wives, children, grandparents, uncles, aunts, nephews, nieces, cousins: Who lives in a house? Composed and recomposed, the notion of family varies according to culture, like the appreciation of degrees of kinship. But how was architecture able to respond to these different familial structures and to divide the space? Whatever the symbolic explanations, it is true that order is often a sure value within the house. The Mongols go so far as to govern the position of the sleepers in the *gher*. If the living space is not divided by partitions, setting boundaries for your corner requires making some arrangements. Sleeping space was formerly organized around the woman, who could have several husbands. On one side, the children slept closest to the fire; the baby snuggled up with her. On the other side—as if the collective imagination split the woman in two parts, two functions, maternal and sexual—the husband and other men of the family slept. The farther they were from her, the weaker their lines of kinship. To express the idea of a split body, the people refer to a husband "of the thighs," a husband "of the head," and a husband "of the ribs."

And in African villages, how do you make spouses and co-spouses of a polygamist husband live together successfully? Scholar Amos Rapaport, who has analyzed the shape of the house from a sociocultural perspective, reports that in this case, the head of the family does not really have a dwelling. Every day, he visits one of his spouses. In Cameroon, concessions are organized around the granaries holding vital foodstuffs, in front of which the women's houses are spread in a circle so that each can access it. The hut of the first spouse is closest to the entrance.

Russia, Siberia, Yamal region. An extended family, including the grandparents, lives together under the same roof.

Christian Seignobos relates how the women organized themselves in the northern part of the country. The concession, called *ay*, was always the property of a man, either because he inherited it or because he built it himself. Each woman raised her own poultry there and cultivated her parcel of field. To have a granary was, on the other hand, a gauge of fidelity and the privilege of the oldest women. The others, who married young, were prohibited to enter there without the agreement of their husband, who regulated the provisions. Despite these very strict rules, each enjoyed a relative independence to manage her *gadget*, a word that means both *hut* and *women and children*. She received visitors there, cooked meals, and sold beer and other products she made. During the difficult work of grinding, she sang what she had to say. According to the themes of the songs, the protests or satisfactions of one woman for the others were divined, in a very pacific manner to manage tensions, even though in Africa, speech is considered to be a powerful tool. You could also tell how many generations succeeded each other within the enclosure of the concession by counting the ox jaws sacrificed for the celebrations and embedded in the lintel of the entry.

In Greenland, ethnologist Marcel Mauss observed that the houses of the Inuit—tents in summer and longhouses in winter—were intended for only one couple and their children. The family, one and indivisible, shared all their possessions. Furniture was reduced to a strict minimum: only one lamp, one bench, one bed, and a large raised couch, made of leaves covered with skins, at the end of the tent. An exemplary family unit.

Botswana, Kalahari Desert. A Bushmen camp gathers an entire clan together.

Inside, Outside

To whom does the house belong? Even if the walls are often the property of the man, the woman is usually in charge of maintenance. Moreover, on the occasion of marriage—in Mongolia, for example— she frequently takes possession of it.

Does the house itself have a sex, what is its relationship of the mixing of the sexes, and who does what? Many traditional societies have answered these questions in their own way. Thus, in the Mongol language, from the word for tent, *gher*— yurt designating only its location—an entire series of words have been derived. *Ghergii* means woman, or wife; *gher byl*, family; *gher bariq*, set up the tent, or get married. Moreover, to indicate a group of dwellings, one refers to a "city of families" and, it is said that the simplest way to take a census of new marriages is to count the new tents. As the Mongols say, when you enter a gher, you become a woman; when you leave, you become a man. It is the activities in which one partakes, more than it is the lodging itself, that characterize the gher. To take care of the fire and cook is feminine; to take care of the cattle is masculine. Would the domestic tasks then be carried out indifferently by either sex, provided that they find themselves indoors or outdoors? For the Kabyle in North Africa, in any case, the differences are clearly marked. Inside is the domain of women, outside, the domain of men. And to those who do not leave the house at the crowing of the cock, watch out, because there are rules to respect. The men even sleep outside in summer. Their place is in the field or in the village assembly. Agriculture and politics are the masculine responsibilities. Men should be at the center of social life and make others respect them. These are ancient traditions, of course, but ones that have left their mark in the organization of houses. Even if you are not of Kabyle or Maghrebi origin, to be "a man in the house" still has little value. In any case, in the neighboring Djurdjura Mountains of Algeria, while man's work was accomplished outdoors in daylight, woman's work was done in the privacy of the house. Baby girls' umbilical cords were buried inside, under the loom. A saying sums up this life devoted to the house very well: "The woman has only two dwelling places, the house and the grave."

Opposite: Senegal. In both the interior and exterior, everyone has a well-established place based on his or her gender.

Following pages: India, Rajasthan. Ambiance of the inner courtyard

The Feeling of Welcome

Isolated or integrated, luxurious or austere: what type of room is reserved for guests? Whether a house is distrustful or welcoming is a question of culture, society, and the relationship with the other and the world.

In the religious caste of the Brahmans in India, a special room is reserved to receive those who are not a part of the family; contact with them can taint—through spiritual or even physical impurities. For the Buddhist Mongols, the life of the house is organized around the altar to the ancestors; everyone is placed according to age, sex, and rank. A guest who is a lama or who holds any type of religious power is seated back to the altar, with the head of the house on the right. To let guests know their importance and the pleasure of receiving them, hosts offer tobacco and fermented mare's milk, and seat guests near the chest of precious objects that contains the family silver and the head of the household's clothes. This place is often located in the north part of the tent, and the male guest gets there by passing through the men's part of the tent, on the west side. The older he is, the wiser he is thought to be, and therefore he must be physically elevated in the image of his social condition, in an arrangement around the cardinal points going from south to north. According to ethnologist Bernard Dupaigne, who wrote about the nomads of Asia, visitors should not enter the tent with a whip—a gesture considered to be an offense—or with their heads covered. They should be careful to sit down quickly so as not to be at the same height as the host. Women and young girls sit with the left leg back and the right knee raised. Men sit with the right leg on the ground, the other raised. Elderly and important people sit cross-legged.

In the Himalaya, guests take a place on a low bench covered with a rug. They also take care—as do many Buddhists—not to offend the divinities of the house and do not cross over the red square, in the middle of which is the central post. This ritual distribution of dwelling space is also found in Madagascar, where "that which faces the west," located where the sun sets, is named the choice spot. There is often an entrance to the north of the house reserved for visitors, and there is a sacred wall to the northeast.

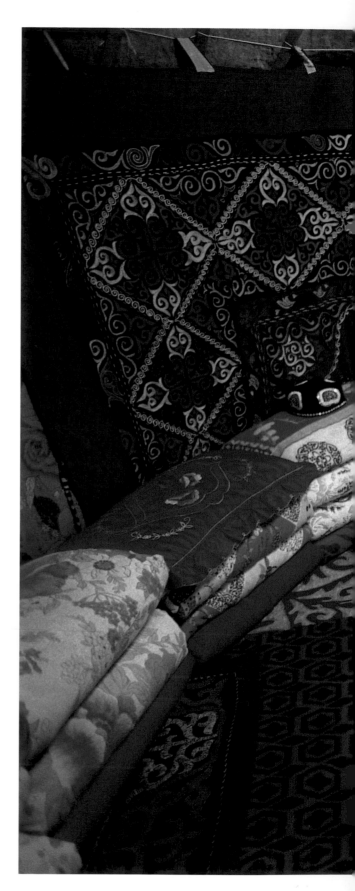

China. Knowing where to seat guests corresponds to a sacred organization of the space.

China, Beijing. Collection of *penzai*. The Chinese have been growing trees in pots since the third century BC.

Interior Beauty

Tapestries, reproductions of landscapes, and mosaics with floral patterns have given splendor and style to the art of living indoors. Plants, from the Greek acanthus to the Egyptian palm tree, have always decorated houses and temples. Materials can be borrowed from nature without remorse when it involves a few trees parsimoniously chopped down close to construction sites. But luxury has a price, and the exotic wood of Western furniture has sometimes contributed to the deforestation of some species of trees. In the sixteenth century, the builders of Moroccan palaces bartered sugar in exchange for Italian marble. Precious silks, crystal chandeliers, wrought-iron balconies, traditional decorations of *zelliges*, green-tiled roofs: the luxury of princely mansions is a sign of power. *Jamurs*—poles decorated with copper balls of different sizes, set up like finials—add the finishing touch. More modest owners must make do with a few spots of color provided by artisanal fabrics, pottery, and by various utilitarian objects skillfully ordered to give modest harmony to the entire room. A few potted plants can also be added to make the temporary enclosure between four walls more tolerable. In China, it is beneficial to have a small tangerine tree, a sign of wealth and peace. With their same desire to bring nature into the house, the Chinese became masters in the art of flower arrangement, setting up miniature gardens, or cultivating *penzai*, dwarf trees in pots. This infatuation with reproducing nature in an ideal way has influenced the furnishing of houses. Console tables—on which the plant world sits on a plate with rocky landscapes sprinkled with temples and small bridges—have become as necessary as the well-known ceramic vases of Chinese craftsmen. The Red Guard of the Cultural Revolution treated this passion as a sign of luxury—just planting flowers could be considered a revolutionary act.

The Choice Rooms

If human beings all have their place in the house, why should it be different for domestic animals? The microcosm reproduced in the house defines, for the Mongols, the place where women take care of the "cold muzzles," or cows, and the men attend to the "hot muzzles," or horses. Milking is done in the northeast, corresponding to the women's interior part of the house, and the raising of stallions, mares, and ponies is done in the southwest, the men's area. In Algeria, peasants have the custom of calling the place where the sheep are penned the "house of beasts." A highly symbolic name, making it clear that the status of animals in the house is equal or nearly equal to that of human beings. In any case, they represent precious goods to which special attention is paid. The Masai shepherds of Kenya share this idea. They actually organize their campsite in a circle around the animals, as a way of protecting them, and showing that they are in the center of their lives. Their nomad unit, called a *kraal*, can be recognized by its circle of thorny hedges surrounding the camp. The kraal brings together an aged man, his wives, and the families of their sons. The animals carry a great deal more than a material value for the Masai shepherds; they govern all their social and spiritual organization. Isn't it said that "a man without a herd is not a man"? Thanks to this proverb, children learn very early about the secular line connecting them to the cattle, and both boys and girls

India, Thar Desert. In the house itself or slightly removed, a room is always reserved for the animals.

will have the responsibility of caring for them when they are adolescents.

In Cameroon, the ox, a symbol of prestige, enjoys a hut all to itself. The Mofus keep a hut for their oxen in the enclosure of their concessions. This requires some architectural arrangements, because the hut can only be closed once the animal has been put in. And it will not leave until a few years later, when, fattened up, it will be sacrificed during a ritual celebration, a kind of chosen ox whose treat-ment resembles that of the bovine of the Japanese breeders of Kobe. These animals also have their own dwelling, a stable removed from agitation and stress, in which they are massaged while classical music is played. The tasty meat of this animal is eaten in shabu-shabu, a type of fondue for the New Year's celebrations, which are also celebrations of the household. Raised inside or outside the house, to the north or the east, for a sacrifice or celebra-tion, the ox often ends up on a plate!

Above: Tanzania, Rift Valley, Oldonio Lengai volcano. A *kraal*, an enclosure made of a thorny hedge, beside a Masai dwelling

Following pages: India, Karnataka. Inner courtyard of a traditional house, where cows and people find shade

China, Beijing. At the end of the day, birds are taken for a walk in their cages.

Infinitely Small

Besides housing men and women, the lodging in the countryside usually shelters a few companions: dogs, cats, fowl, and cattle. The Korowais, in their perched huts in New Guinea, even have small tame pigs that they offer at marriages or to strengthen good-neighbor relationships. But the prize for originality goes to the Chinese, because even though the cricket is a tiny animal, raising it in a cage is a great art. As the proverb goes, "You always have room for one more in your home," and the Chinese have always had an interest in the infinitely small. In the seventh century, crickets became a part of the Chinese household, a custom that spread to Japan a few centuries later. There are many different kinds: black, yellow, green; some are aggressive, some are excellent singers. Whatever the type, odes have always been composed to them. Recorded by Michel Culas, a specialist in Chinese objects, this poem testifies to the devoted attachment to these insects, which are symbols of summer: "They live out in the open during the seventh moon, come near to houses during the eighth, sing in front of the door in the ninth, and hide under the bed during the tenth." Practical manuals for raising crickets have been widespread in literature. The first was written by Jia Setao, minister of the Emperor Lizong in the thirteenth century. He set down crickets' habits, rearing, training, and care with a rare meticulousness. Legend tells that this learned man, who had an entire cricket collection, met a tragic end. He was so engrossed in his passion for crickets that he was condemned to death for ignoring the affairs of the state. But not all Chinese went this far, and many had a cricket at home to create a relaxing atmosphere.

Raising birds was also an activity very prized by the Chinese nobility, who devoted as much time to it as their *penzai*. Today in Beijing, this tradition can still be seen when, at the end of the day, people take their birds outside for some fresh air.

And, in the end, isn't putting a fish in a bowl more original than shutting a rabbit in a hutch? In Asia, this peaceful spectacle is appreciated, and the red fish is always a good omen for the house.

Pets

"Beware of dog." If this warning has a dissuasive effect, it's because nothing seems to equal a flesh and blood guardian, with its teeth and claws. (Or, if you prefer the quacking of a white goose to spirited barking, with its beak and feathers.) When it is not happy with a niche on the front steps, the dog's place is often inside, near the inhabitants, where some superstitions study its smallest actions and movements, sometimes reading in them the destiny of the house. In Mongolia, the dog is the only domesticated animal to which the nomads give a name. It is often the mascot of the family, and to see it abruptly leave camp is a bad omen. On the other hand, the arrival of a neighbor's dog in the *gher* foretells a happy event. Because it is so close to people, a great deal of importance is attached to the dog. It is even thought that if a dog is buried with its tail cut off, it will return in human form. Many mythologies, from Anubis to Cerberus, refer to the dog. Associated with invisible forces and the divinities, it often symbolizes the earth, water, and moon. Therefore, it is not surprising that the human loves the company of the dog. In China, where it is painted or carved on doors, it can protect the dwelling.

The dog, which can evoke fear, is somewhat like the cat, to which a dual character is assigned according to events and civilizations. In the Maghrebi countryside, seeing a cat enter the house with a piece of wool or a feather on its back means that one will soon be visited by guests to whom meat must be offered. The sight of a cat going toward the stable indicates that one will buy a cow, if it is spring, or an ox, if it is the time of plowing. Muslims often consider the cat beneficial, but if it is completely black it becomes the incarnation of a jinni, an evil spirit. The cat can also be the incarnation of an evil spirit in Japan, while in Cambodia, it is associated with original chaos. A ritual that consisted of passing a cat in a cage from house to house, then putting water on it, was thought to favor rain, and thus make the fields more fertile—an image more complex than that of a sleeping Western tomcat, tranquilly stretched out on the sofa, a symbol of nonchalant serenity.

Indonesia, Irian Jaya. A Korowai woman and her dog climb into their dwelling 13 feet (4 meters) above the marshlands.

China. In the Uighour
Muslim community, a meal
shared by women

Inside Rules

A house is not an empty shell. It is often part of a genealogy, including ancestors and illustrious owners. It represents the continuity of family history. Therefore, the house has a life, and if the inhabitants don't want to see it haunted by spirits of ancestors or protective divinities, it is better to respect ancestral taboos.

Spreading blood on the walls is the foremost of all prohibitions. (Particularly the blood from a crime, because assassins are very superstitious, like everyone else.) Killing an individual in his or her house, especially in front of his or her mother and sister, was long thought a sure way to break the magic circle that surrounded the dwelling—and to curse it. This was believed for a long time in tribal regions before people were organized into states with a justice system and courts. Menstrual blood was to be avoided as much as possible. Women often stayed in other lodgings during this time and when they reached puberty.

The house is not a place where anyone can just walk in. In the countryside of Algeria, very strict regulations determined who could or could not penetrate there. A distinction was made between the "central post" family, i.e., those with a lineage from the grandmother, and the "girder," those connected to the grandfather. The former had to be content with visiting occasionally, while the latter had the privilege of living there. Things became more complicated when one of the male or female heads of the family died. For example, an uncle could not sleep at his nephew's house when his sister was no longer alive, and the parents-in-law of one of the family members had to be announced. Therefore, it was necessary to be perfectly aware of the usage and customs so as not to commit any social blunders. For strangers, the situation was very clear: they were not allowed to enter. The visitor was instead received by the village chief according to his rank and lodged in the mosque.

Who ate with whom was also one of the big questions in a house, because in many societies men and women took their meals separately. This practice was often linked to the fear of incest, especially when food was shared with the fingers.

Strange Cohabitation

Many believe that there are numerous spirits in a house. The visible beings are not the only occupants. Most often, spirits live with the inhabitants. These supernatural beings have their assigned place in traditional societies. They are respected and sacrifices—of a chicken or a cock—are offered to them. The end result is always the same, i.e., the integrity of the house and of the inhabitants is preserved, because what affects one rebounds on other. In Japan, care is taken never to disturb Zashiki Warashi. This imaginary creature enters houses in the form of a child and brings happiness and prosperity. Its presence is noticed when the inhabitants have the feeling that objects have been moved around and when the floorboards crack. Its departure brings about the decline of the family. And if the saying "a healthy soul in a healthy body" is accurate, a healthy house is also necessary to guard a healthy body. The Hmong of Thailand understand this. Added to the fear of sickness and death is their fear of seeing their house, which is made of boards or bamboo with a roof of thatch or wooden tiles, destroyed by violent rains or a gust of wind. Thus, the spirit of the door is very important. Every year, the father opens the door during a ritual ceremony, so that prosperity, health, and longevity can enter. Moreover, they are verbally invited in. Sickness can only enter the body through the orifices, and misfortune through the house's door. Thus, a wooden sword is placed inside, just over the entrance beam, to keep away evil spirits.

In India, sitting on the threshold of the house is not recommended: boils will appear on the part of the body that has been in contact with it, a punishment imposed by the spirits of the premises. For the Serers of Africa, to combat evil and make it leave the body, the odor of the house must be pestilential. A few branches soaked in excrement and placed above the threshold should make evil leave or stop it from entering. What happens symbolically in the house is important, as a very human way of learning to deal with sickness, suffering, and death.

Opposite: Indonesia, Celebs, Toraja country, Palawa. The horns of buffalo that are sacrificed in ceremonies mark the boundaries of the village's sacred space.

Following pages: Côte d'Ivoire, Senufo village of Niofoin. Sacred hut reserved for fetishes

The Honored

To join the community of divinities is a desire of the dead in China. Though the dead sometimes attain celestial status, they possess, nonetheless, one choice place, in the form of tablets, in a corner of the dwelling. If the inhabitants want the deceased to be concerned with the destiny of the house, offerings of food and drink, consecrated to the departed, are placed in front of the altar. Incense, candles, and three cups of tea are placed there on the first and fifteenth day of the lunar month. This is a way of maintaining a connection with the departed, an idea shared by many Buddhist cultures, where death is often presented in the core of life. The spirits of the dead are also associated with banquets that follow important events such as marriages, births, successful exams, and social promotions.

The anniversaries of deaths, every three, seven, forty-three, and fifty years, are always the occasion of a family meal in Japan. Everyone gathers in front of the *butsudan*, a large lacquered and gold-plated altar several tatamis wide. Since an imperial decree in the seventh century AD solicited the usage of this altar, it has had its place in the house. Funeral tablets called *ihai* contain the names of the dead beside their photographs.

Cambodia. Family altar
honoring ancestors and
Buddhist divinities

In Africa, ancestors' altars are also found in the huts of traditional villages. For the mountain people of Cameroon, altars are marked by pieces of pottery or shards called *kouli*. They are usually found in the concession's vulnerable points. At the death of a head of the family, the father replaces the grandfather on the altar and, in this way, the generations follow one after the other.

For the Malgasy of Madagascar, the northeast corner of the house is sacred. Shelves are built there for offerings in honor of the dead. The dwellings are organized according to the stars: they are divided into twelve parts that correspond to the months of the year. Each section has a very precise assignment, like the storing of rice or water. The position of the bodies on the inside also obeys a religious representation. Thus, the bed is always to the east, the head to the north, and the doors and windows to the west. In the Tibetan Himalaya, the ancestors and divinities' altar often divides the space when the house does not have a central post, which is considered sacred. Women stay to its left to cook, and to its right, the family and guests restore themselves under the beneficial influence of the ancestors.

Russia, Tuva. Hanging photographs of ancestors on the walls is a way of honoring them.

Household Gods

India, Ladakh, Zanskar. The lama has come to meditate near the family altar.

The Setsobon is celebrated in Japan during the first week of February. It marks the arrival of spring according to the ancient lunar calendar. "The demon leaves, luck arrives." Such phrases were used to purify the house while throwing grilled soy grains outside. Getting rid of evil consisted of sending into the beyond the soul of the departed, which transformed into an ogre that came to avenge the injustices endured during their lifetime. With two horns, three eyes, three clawed toes, and a red face, this legendary creature could invite itself into your home if you were not on your guard. Fortunately, the house was in the competent hands of the household gods for the rest of the year. The Seven Gods of Good Fortune sat enthroned in the kitchen on a shelf, from where they were thought to watch over the family. Sake, rice, *kaki*s, and tangerines made up their daily food.

The Chinese always celebrate the New Year with a lot of noise and chase away evil spirits with an annual cleaning. Plaits of firecrackers on a cane have been specially designed to explode indoors, in front of the effigy of the Spirit of the Hearth. Zao-jun, or Tsao-chen, the divinity linked to the hearth, was imprinted on a stamp and glued on top of the stove. A little before the end of the year, the divinity departed to see the Jade Emperor, the supreme ruler who assured the proper workings of the universe. In the Chinese conception, the life beyond was managed almost exactly like life on earth. It followed a very strict hierarchical organization, with the same bothersome administrative protocol, so that the spirit had to constantly go to its superiors over the least human occurrence. The prime minister and divine civil servants were in charge of calculating the destiny, the portion of chance and evil, and the merit and posterity due to each individual on earth. This was no doubt a colossal undertaking. And so that the report on loved ones was softened, each family tried to bribe their household god by offering it a meal. It seems that sweets were the most appreciated of the offerings. It was said that sweets could perhaps "seal" the lips of the god. In India, where the gods all gathered together in the kitchen, the most sacred room of the house, they were venerated throughout the year in the hope that they would improve daily life.

The Living and the Dead

According to archeologists, it appears that since the Neolithic period, beginning around 10,000 BC, sepulchers were associated with the house, at least in the Middle East. At that time, humans had already been burying their dead for one hundred thousand years. Religious practice, belief in an afterlife, or the hope of keeping memory alive: it is difficult to know what this represented in human thought. But a vision of the world was taking shape. Mythologies, often announcing the importance of fertility and maternity, were developed as a way of explaining the inexplicable, and to ease the fear of death. It was often believed that the spirit of the departed was better off at home, and the dead were buried in the basement of their house.

This practice is found in many cultures today. The position of the body in the house is significant for mourning. After having closed the dead person's eyes and covered the body with white linen, the Lao of Southeast Asia place the deceased in the same direction as the house frame. Since their dwelling is usually placed in the same direction as a course of sacred water, the body is actually placed in relationship to the stream. The Mekong River formerly played this role of religious reference. It was thought that the dead had to leave the house "feet first" and through the facade. When the architecture did not permit the inhabitants to conform to ritual traditions, a temporary ladder was built called the "ladder of death."

Even Kabyle funeral chants in Algeria compare the tomb to a house. They evoke the "house under the earth" and describe the erecting of walls and the sculpting of clay benches. The body is washed at the stable entrance, a dark part of the house. The Bonzes of Southeast Asia allocate the space for the funeral ceremony according to special rules; they place themselves in the easternmost part of the house, with the person presiding to the northeast, as close as possible to the statue of Buddha. The oldest men of the assembly face the monks, while those of the following generation are behind them, and so on. The women, grouped from grandmothers to granddaughters, accompany the men to the west, toward the kitchen.

In Syria, though the dead were previously buried inside, today they can also be buried outside between two houses, or even with the skull on one side (like religious furnishings) not far from the hearth, and the body on the other side. The Buddhist culture shares a similar practice, wherein the ashes of the dead are spread over several different places: in the former domicile, in a nearby cemetery, or in the place the parents were buried. Whatever the practice, it is certain that humanity has not stopped meditating on the mortal condition. By constantly reasserting the symbolic link between the living and the dead, by including death in the core of daily life in the house, we have demonstrated that we are something more than animals.

Togo, Tamberma country.
Even the dead have their
place in the house thanks
to altars that honor the
souls of ancestors.

Photograph Credits

Project Manager, English-language edition: Susan Richmond
Editor, English-language edition: Carrie Hornbeck
Jacket design, English-language edition: Michael J. Walsh Jr and Arlene Lee
Design Coordinator, English-language edition: Arlene Lee
Production Coordinator, English-language edition: Kaija Markoe

Library of Congress Cataloging-in-Publication Data

Laffon, Martine.
[Habitat du monde English]
A home in the world : houses and cultures / Martine and Caroline Laffon ;
translated from the French by Lenora Ammon.
p. cm.
Includes bibliographical references and index.
ISBN 0-8109-5607-1 (hardcover)
1. Dwellings. 2. Vernacular architecture. 3. Architecture, Domestic. I. Laffon, Caroline. II. Title.

GT165.L35 2004
392.3'6—dc22
2004009768

Copyright © 2004 Éditions de La Martinière, Paris
English translation copyright © 2004 Harry N. Abrams, Inc.

Printed and bound in Italy
10 9 8 7 6 5 4 3 2 1

Harry N. Abrams, Inc.
100 Fifth Avenue
New York, N.Y. 10011
www.abramsbooks.com

Abrams is a subsidiary of
LA MARTINIÈRE